I0701138

This book is dedicated to Community Action, the movement that opened a door when I needed one, offered opportunity instead of judgment, and made it possible for me to move from client, to first job, to a career I love deeply.

I am profoundly grateful to the many people who believed in me along the way: the frontline staff who showed compassion and dignity in moments that mattered, the supervisors and mentors who took chances and set high expectations, and the colleagues who modeled what principled, community-centered leadership looks like in practice. Your support shaped not only my career, but my understanding of service, accountability, and hope.

Please consider this book my way of giving back to the sector that invests in people, builds pathways to stability, and proves every day that opportunity changes lives when it is paired with trust and leadership.

Contents

Nonprofit Navigation

A Nonprofit Field Guide

Introduction

Why I Wrote This Book, and Why It Matters Now

Over the past thirty years, I've built a career in nonprofit leadership that spans direct service, program development, executive management, board governance, and community advocacy. Like many who find their way into this work, I didn't set out to lead a nonprofit organization—I found myself drawn into it by a combination of values, opportunity, and a deep sense of responsibility. That blend of purpose and pragmatism is something I see often in nonprofit professionals. It's also what inspired me to write this book.

This text was born from a recurring conversation I've had with emerging and mid-career leaders: "Where can I go to learn how to do this right?" Not just the basics of grant writing or how to read a budget, but the full spectrum of skills needed to lead an organization with integrity, strategy, and resilience. Too often, those answers are scattered across dense academic texts, short-term workshops, and the informal wisdom of mentors—when it's available at all. I wanted to create something different: a comprehensive, accessible, and field-informed guide to nonprofit leadership.

As I developed the structure of this book, I considered what I wished I had known earlier in my career. I also considered what today's leaders need to know to lead effectively in a world marked by uncertainty, inequality, and rapid change. The result is a textbook that combines theory with practice, strategy with empathy, and structure with adaptability. It reflects the values that drive our sector while also equipping readers with the tools to meet the real demands of leadership today.

The Evolution of Leadership in the Nonprofit Sector

The nonprofit sector has changed dramatically in recent decades. We've seen exponential growth in the number of registered nonprofits, increasing competition for funding, and rising expectations around outcomes, transparency, and accountability. Leaders are no longer expected to simply manage programs—they are called upon to navigate complex systems, build coalitions, guide diverse teams, and engage in deep strategic thinking.

At the same time, communities have grown more diverse, social movements more urgent, and stakeholder expectations more nuanced. Donors want to know their gifts are making a measurable impact. Boards want to understand risk, sustainability, and strategic direction. Frontline staff need support, clarity, and inclusive leadership. And the communities we serve want to be seen, heard, and respected—not just helped.

The COVID-19 pandemic underscored these demands. In a matter of weeks, nonprofit leaders had to pivot operations, adopt new technologies, triage staff well-being, and address rapidly changing community needs. Those who had already built adaptive systems, strong communication practices, and collaborative cultures weathered the storm more effectively than those who had not. The experience exposed a broader truth: in today's environment, technical knowledge isn't enough. Nonprofit leaders must be emotionally intelligent, culturally competent, ethically grounded, and digitally literate.

A Book That Reflects the Work

Nonprofit Navigator is designed to reflect this complexity and prepare leaders for the realities of the field. The book is structured around the core competencies I've seen time and again as necessary for success:

Strategic Leadership: Balancing long-term vision with day-to-day execution.

Financial Stewardship: Building and managing budgets that support—not just track—the mission.

Ethical Practice: Navigating gray areas with transparency and integrity.

Fundraising Strategy: Connecting with donors in ways that foster long-term relationships.

Program Design and Evaluation: Creating programs that are responsive, sustainable, and accountable to the communities they serve.

Crisis Management: Leading through uncertainty with composure, communication, and care.

Change Management: Helping organizations evolve while maintaining stability and trust.

Each section draws from real-world examples, current research, and the lived experiences of nonprofit professionals. I've included case studies, discussion prompts, and applied tools to help translate theory into action. My goal is not just to inform—it is to equip.

You'll also find special attention paid to the skills that too often get sidelined in leadership development programs: cultural competence, digital fluency, and emotional intelligence. These aren't "soft skills." They are leadership essentials. When we fail to center them, we risk undermining our own effectiveness and eroding trust with our stakeholders.

Why I Teach—and Why I Keep Learning

Writing this book coincides with a new chapter in my own professional journey: teaching a community college course on nonprofit leadership. In preparing to teach, I realized there wasn't a single resource that captured both the breadth and nuance of what I wanted my students to learn. I wanted to offer more than theory. I wanted to prepare them for what it feels like to lead in this space—the emotional labor, the ethical dilemmas, the creative problem-solving, and the moments of transformation that remind us why this work matters.

My students come from a wide range of backgrounds: some are current nonprofit professionals, others are new to the field, and many are navigating life circumstances that make their voices especially valuable in shaping the future of our sector. They bring lived experience, community insight, and a desire to lead with purpose. This book is written with them in mind—and with you, the reader, in mind as well.

Whether you're reading this as part of a course, on your own time, or alongside your colleagues in a leadership cohort, I hope it serves as both a practical guide and a thoughtful companion. I hope it challenges you to think critically, act courageously, and lead with compassion and clarity. I hope it helps you see yourself not just as a manager of tasks, but as a steward of people, mission, and community trust.

What to Expect as You Read

Each section of the book builds on the last, beginning with an overview of the nonprofit sector and progressing through topics like budgeting, fundraising, program planning, needs assessment, outcome measurement, and change leadership. The final section invites you to reflect on your own leadership journey and to apply what you've learned through a capstone project or organizational initiative.

Throughout the book, you'll find:

1. Real-world case studies that illustrate key points.

2. Glossaries and key terms to build your fluency in sector-specific language.

3. Discussion questions and activities to support individual learning and group dialogue.

4. Sidebars and checklists to support quick application and review.

5. Instructor-friendly layouts for those using this book in academic or training settings.

The tone is formal enough to serve in a college classroom, yet conversational enough to remain accessible. I've made a point to avoid jargon when plain language suffices. And I've worked hard to center equity, ethics, and community in every chapter—not as standalone topics, but as through-lines across the leadership journey.

A Final Note

The decision to lead in the nonprofit sector is not always easy. It rarely comes with glamorous perks or guaranteed outcomes. But for those of us called to this work, it is deeply meaningful. We get to hold hope in hard places. We get to solve problems that matter. We get to help communities thrive.

Leadership in this space is not about perfection. It's about showing up with integrity, learning as you go, and building systems that reflect the values you stand for. That's what this book is about.

Thank you for doing this work. Thank you for seeking to do it well. And thank you for trusting this book to help you along the way.

Let's begin.

- Chapter 1 -

Introduction to Nonprofit Leadership

In this opening chapter we build the conceptual foundation for everything that follows. You will first situate today's nonprofit enterprise in its historical continuum, then assess its economic and social footprint, examine the characteristics that distinguish mission-driven organizations; and finally analyze the emerging trends reshaping twenty-first century practice. The chapter closes by linking these sector dynamics to the adaptive leadership skills you will hone throughout the text.

Learning Objectives

By the end of Chapter 1 readers will be able to:

1. Trace four major eras in the evolution of the U.S. nonprofit sector and explain how each era reshaped governance and funding norms.

2. Interpret current labor market and GDP data to articulate the sector's macroeconomic significance. Too much

3. Distinguish nonprofits from public and private sector entities in terms of legal, financial, and mission dimensions, and identify where a given organization sits on the lifecycle curve.

4. Critically evaluate the contemporary challenges of digital transformation, equity imperatives, climate resilience, and regulatory technology and propose evidence-based responses.

5. Integrate systems thinking, emotional intelligence, and clear ethical perspective into a coherent leadership framework suited to complex, resource constrained environments.

6. Formulate plausible scenarios for the sector's future direction to 2035 and identify the leadership capacities required to thrive in each.

Quick-Glance Map of Chapter 1

Section	Learning Objectives
Historical Evolution	Trace sector eras and governance shifts
Economic & Social Footprint	Interperet economic data
Defining Characteristics	Distinguish nonprofits and lifecycle
Modern Trends & Challenges	Evaluate contemporary challenges
Intersection with Leadership	Integrate adaptive leadership framework
Future Trajectories	Formulate 2035 scenarios

Historical Evolution of the Nonprofit Sector

The nonprofit sector in the U.S. has evolved over centuries, influenced by cultural values, political movements, and economic conditions. Understanding this evolution helps today's leaders recognize how past efforts continue to influence governance models, funding strategies, and public expectations.

Historically, the nonprofit sector can trace its roots to philanthropic efforts dating back several centuries, evolving significantly through faith-based institutions, charitable trusts/foundations, and voluntary associations. In the US, the establishment of nonprofits gained momentum in the 19th century, driven by social reforms aimed at alleviating poverty, promoting education, and improving access to healthcare. The sector expanded most notably in the 20th century, especially following World War II, as economic prosperity combined with societal awareness fueled the growth of civil rights movements, environmental activism, and healthcare advancements.

Pre-19th Century Philanthropy

Philanthropy prior to the 1800s was largely rooted in religious and communal traditions. In colonial America, churches, mutual aid societies, and voluntary associations formed the backbone of charitable work. These efforts were localized, often informal, and focused on immediate relief such as food, housing, and burial support (Hall, 2006). Civic duty was intertwined with moral and religious expectations, and leadership often emerged from clergy or respected elders.

19th Century Institutionalization in the U.S.

A significant shift occurred in the 1800s as social reform movements led to more formal organizational structures. Abolitionist, temperance, and women's suffrage movements catalyzed the rise of advocacy-based nonprofits. Simultaneously, the rise of industrial wealth enabled philanthropists such as Andrew Carnegie to fund libraries, universities, and foundations, formalizing large-scale charitable giving (Bremner, 1988). Nonprofit governance began adopting boards, bylaws, and strategic planning all of which are hallmarks of today's practice.

Post-WWII Expansion & Civil Rights Era

After World War II, U.S. nonprofits experienced rapid growth. The GI Bill, civil rights legislation, and the War on Poverty expanded federal investment in social services, often delivered through nonprofits. During this era, community action agencies and legal aid groups emerged to address systemic inequalities (Salamon, 2012). The civil rights movement also catalyzed grassroots leadership and nonprofit accountability to marginalized communities.

Twenty-First Century Globalization

Globalization, technological innovation, and the rise of transnational advocacy have redefined the sector since 2000. Many nonprofits now operate across borders, address global issues such as climate change and human trafficking, and use digital platforms to mobilize support. Regulatory environments have become more complex, requiring nonprofit leaders to understand international funding, data privacy laws, and cross-cultural engagement (Anheier, 2014).

Comparative Vignette: Global Nonprofit Trajectories

While the U.S. nonprofit sector has followed a largely privatized, service-delivery model, other regions have developed distinct approaches reflecting their histories and governance systems.

In the European Union, nonprofits, often called civil society organizations, are closely integrated with public systems. Many EU countries fund nonprofits as extensions of state welfare programs, resulting in more centralized oversight and stable funding. For example, in Sweden and Germany, nonprofit elder care and social housing programs are heavily subsidized and are subject to public accountability standards (Salamon & Sokolowski, 2016).

By contrast, Latin America has a vibrant tradition of community-based organizing rooted in liberation theology, human rights defense, and resistance to authoritarian regimes. In countries like Brazil and Chile, NGOs often emerged during political repression to serve as platforms for civic expression. Today, Latin American nonprofits blend service delivery with social justice advocacy, although many struggle with unstable funding and donor dependency (Bebbington & Thiele, 1993).

In Sub-Saharan Africa, the nonprofit landscape is shaped by colonial legacies, foreign aid, and urgent development needs. Many organizations are donor-driven NGOs focusing on health, education, or disaster relief. Yet indigenous models—such as mutual aid societies and faith-based networks—remain central in rural areas. Leadership must navigate complex power dynamics between international funders and local communities (Fowler, 2000).

These regional contrasts remind us that while the goals of nonprofits may align globally, their pathways, power structures, and funding models reflect local contexts. Effective leaders must understand both historical roots and contemporary trends when engaging across borders.

Year	Event	Leadership Implication
1630s	Founding of religious charities in colonial America	Leadership rooted in moral authority and communal responsibility
1889	Hull House founded by Jane Addams	Rise of professional social work and community-based leadership
1913	IRS tax exemption codified for charities (Revenue Act)	Legal recognition and new accountability structures
1945–65	Postwar expansion and Civil Rights Movement	Growth in advocacy and equity-centered organizational governance
1980s	Reagan-era privatization policies	Increased pressure for nonprofit efficiency and independence

Year	Event	Leadership Implication
2001	Global war on terror reshapes NGO regulations	Heightened scrutiny, compliance requirements, and digital security
2020	COVID-19 pandemic disrupts global service delivery	Demand for digital transformation and crisis-ready leadership

Economic & Social Footprint

The U.S. nonprofit sector exerts a profound influence on both the economy and civil society. According to the latest data from the Bureau of Labor Statistics (2023), the nonprofit workforce accounts for approximately 10.2% of total private employment in the United States, equivalent to over 12.5 million jobs across health, education, social assistance, and other mission-driven fields. This scale positions the nonprofit sector as a formidable economic engine, not only rivaling but surpassing some industries traditionally viewed as primary job creators.

Today, the nonprofit sector remains indispensable within American society, contributing more than $1.2 trillion annually to the economy (Urban Institute, 2022). Nonprofits leverage substantial influence by operating at the intersection of public service delivery, policy advocacy, and community mobilization. Unlike commercial businesses, nonprofits reinvest any surplus revenues directly back into their missions, a fundamental distinction recognized and protected by their tax-exempt status under IRS Code 501(c)(3). This financial structure underscores their accountability not to shareholders, but to the communities and causes that they serve, emphasizing transparency, ethical stewardship, and mission-centric operations.

In terms of economic output, the nonprofit sector contributes approximately 5.6% to the national Gross Domestic Product (GDP), a figure comparable to sectors such as construction or transportation (Bureau of Economic Analysis, 2023). Despite this substantial footprint, the sector remains underrecognized in public discourse relative to its for-profit and governmental counterparts.

Nonprofits in the U.S. address diverse areas, including healthcare, education, environmental sustainability, human rights, and poverty alleviation. They often act in critical capacities, filling service gaps unaddressed by market forces and insufficiently covered by government programs. For example, during the COVID-19 pandemic, nonprofits provided roughly 40% of community health services in underserved regions, demonstrating remarkable resilience, adaptability, and innovation in crisis response (WHO, 2023).

What is SROI?

Social Return on Investment (SROI) is an evaluative approach that assigns financial proxies to social outcomes, enabling stakeholders to compare the social impact of programs to the resources invested.

1. **Quick Example 1:** A youth mentorship program that reduces high school dropout rates by 30% among at-risk students may save the public education system thousands in remediation and generate long-term economic benefits via higher earning potential.

2. **Quick Example 2:** A community health clinic's vaccination outreach reduces emergency department visits, decreasing taxpayer-funded health expenditures and improving local workforce productivity.

According to the Independent Sector (2021), high-performing

nonprofits can deliver between \$2 to \$7 in social value for every dollar spent, underscoring the sector's cost-effectiveness and catalytic potential.

In sum, the nonprofit sector is more than a philanthropic endeavor—it is an essential component of national stability and societal well-being. Understanding its economic scale and social impact equips future leaders to advocate for appropriate recognition, investment, and policy support.

Defining Characteristics of Nonprofits

Nonprofits are distinguished by a few fundamental pillars:

1. **Mission Centricity:** Nonprofits maintain a clear, defined mission aimed at providing public benefit. Whether reducing homelessness, advancing education, or protecting the environment, each programmatic decision and organizational strategy aligns closely with the mission statement. This mission-focused approach helps maintain organizational coherence and ethical accountability.

2. **Governance Structure:** Governance in nonprofits involves oversight by a board of directors responsible for fiduciary stewardship, strategic guidance, and ensuring mission fidelity. Effective governance practices, as outlined by Lester Salamon (2017), include transparent decision-making processes, regular evaluation, and responsive leadership capable of adapting to changing societal expectations and regulatory requirements.

3. **Funding Diversity:** The financial stability of nonprofits often hinges on their ability to diversify revenue sources, ranging from grants and donations to earned income and government contracts. Successful nonprofit leaders must skillfully balance financial strategies, prioritizing ethical stewardship

while ensuring the sustainability and scalability of programs.

Organizational Lifecycle Stages

Nonprofit organizations, like living systems, evolve through distinct lifecycle stages, each presenting unique leadership, funding, and governance demands. Recognizing where an organization stands on this curve helps leaders to anticipate challenges and allocate resources strategically.

Startup Stage

Newly formed nonprofits are often driven by visionary founders addressing unmet needs. Governance tends to be informal, with early boards acting more as volunteer workgroups than fiduciary stewards. The primary focus is on legal formation, mission articulation, and early program development. Leaders must balance passion with structure, establishing foundational policies and financial systems to support sustainability (Anheier, 2014).

Growth Stage

During this phase, the organization expands programs, formalizes staffing, and diversifies revenue. Governance becomes more professionalized, with boards evolving into strategic partners. Leaders must shift from doing to delegating, requiring skills in performance management, fundraising strategy, and compliance. At this stage, tension often arises between rapid scaling and maintaining mission fidelity.

Maturity Stage

Established nonprofits benefit from stable infrastructure, recognized brand identity, and predictable funding. However, maturity may breed complacency. Effective governance during this phase includes rigorous program evaluation, leadership succession planning, and risk management. Boards and executives must remain outward facing, scanning for emerging needs and opportunities to innovate before stagnation sets in (Crutchfield & Grant, 2012).

Turnaround or Closure Stage

Organizations facing declining relevance, financial distress, or leadership vacuums enter a renewal or closure phase. In turnaround scenarios, leaders are tasked with reengaging stakeholders, eliminating inefficiencies, and possibly redefining the mission. When closure becomes necessary, responsible governance requires ethical wind-down practices that honor commitments to staff, clients, and funders. This stage calls for exceptional transparency and adaptive leadership (Herman & Renz, 2020).

Understanding these lifecycle stages equips leaders to assess organizational health and readiness. Governance structures must adapt over time, evolving from founder-led decision-making in the startup phase to policy-driven oversight in maturity. Likewise, leadership must develop flexible competencies to guide the organization through transitions while upholding mission integrity.

Reflection Prompt:

1. Where is your organization on the lifecycle curve?

2. What governance and leadership capacities are most urgent at this stage?

Modern Trends and Challenges

Several critical trends are reshaping the nonprofit sector in contemporary times:

Digital Transformation and Remote Operations in Nonprofit Management

Advances in technology continue to redefine how nonprofits

design, resource, and deliver mission-driven programs. Cloud-based customer relationship management (CRM) apps, AI- assisted donor analytics, virtual volunteering portals, and omnichannel advocacy platforms such as HubSpot have evolved from being "nice-to-have" to operationally imperative. Recent sector polling indicates that 68 % of organizations employ digital advocacy campaigns to mobilize support-ers at scale, while the majority now capture donor journeys inside a unified CRM (Nonprofit Tech for Good, 2023). The result is sharper segmentation, faster feedback loops, and data-driven program pivots that previously required months of manual reporting.

The parallel rise of remote work and virtual meetings has ac-celerated this transformation. On the upside, distributed teams allow nonprofits to recruit specialized talent and volunteers regardless of ge-ography, trim facilities overhead, and sustain service continuity during crises. Hybrid board meetings boost quorum rates and enable more frequent, bite sized governance check-ins, improving fiduciary over-sight. Virtual volunteering further widens participation by removing transportation, childcare, and disability barriers.

Yet the remote model introduces fresh governance and cultural challenges. Unequal broadband access can exclude beneficiaries and frontline staff, while "remote engagement burnout" erodes engage-ment and collaborative creativity. Cyber risk management becomes increasingly complex as home networks become de facto extensions of the organizational perimeter; 54% of nonprofits surveyed in 2024 re-ported at least one phishing incident linked to remote endpoints (Cy-berPeace Institute, 2024). Finally, sustaining mission alignment across dispersed teams demands deliberate investment in digital onboarding, shared metrics, and periodic in person retreats.

Forward-looking leaders must treat technology not as a luxury but as core infrastructure, budgeting for continuous skills develop-ment, inclusive design, and resilience testing to ensure that digital expansion translates into equitable, mission centric outcomes.

Equity Imperatives and Poverty Focused Advocacy in Nonprofit Management

The reckoning sparked by the 2020 racial justice uprisings forced nonprofits to critically examine not only their staffing patterns, but their program theory as well: Are we alleviating symptoms or dismantling root causes? In practice, that has meant elevating diversity, equity, and inclusion (DEI) from an HR initiative to a governing value that shapes grant criteria, board composition, and community accountability structures. A 2021 National Council of Nonprofits survey found that 74 % of institutional donors now screen for explicit DEI commitments before releasing funds. By 2024, 59 % of U.S. human services charities reported retooling their logic models to address structural drivers of poverty such as housing segregation, wage stagnation, and educational inequity (Urban Institute, 2024).

Federal priorities have since pivoted toward "equal opportunity," compelling organizations that rely on public contracts to translate value-laden DEI language into compliance-oriented metrics, without diluting intent. Astute leaders map each poverty-reduction objective to a policy lever: affordable housing regulation, Medicaid expansion, or living wage mandates. They then deploy multi-tier advocacy, employing grassroots storytelling, data visualizations, and coalition lobbying to influence statutes while continuing to deliver direct relief. Feeding America, for instance, pairs meal distribution with federal SNAP lobbying, illustrating a twin track of relief and reform.

The equity agenda also exposes internal tensions: staff from marginalized communities may question why leadership diversity lags behind program policy, while rural clients balk at language perceived to be elitist. Addressing such friction demands transparent pay scales, participatory budgeting, and messaging that frames equity, not as charity, but as systemic fairness. Nonprofits that transcend mere compliance by embedding DEI/equal opportunity metrics in governance are better poised to eradicate, not simpley ameliorate, poverty's structural causes.

Public Trust Erosion and Systemic Mistrust in Human Service Funding

Polarized politics and sensationalized media coverage have magnified isolated nonprofit missteps into a wider narrative that "the system can't be trusted." Edelman's 2023 Trust Barometer shows U.S. confidence in charities dropping from 70 % in 2018 to 57 %—the steepest decline among all sectors. State and federal committees increasingly cite this erosion to justify trimming human services appropriations, asserting that private philanthropy or market solutions can shoulder the load. Reduced public investment then shrinks program reach, deepening service gaps and, in turn, reinforcing skepticism, generating a destabilizing feedback loop.

Transactional transparency measures, such as posting Form 990s or glossy annual reports are no longer sufficient. Sector leaders are responding with three integrated tactics:

Radical Disclosure: Realtime public dashboards display key outcomes, audit status, and executive pay in plain language. Early adopters like Child Trends report a 22 % boost in donor retention after launching open data portals (Internal Evaluation, 2024).

Independent Assurance: Coalitions commission third-party impact verification via Social Return on Investment (SROI) protocols, reducing doubts about self-reported success.

Reciprocal Storytelling: Beneficiaries coauthor narrative evidence, including critiques, which increases perceived authenticity by 15 % (Stanford Social Innovation Review, 2024).

Critically, executives must pair transparency with policy education that reframes public funding as risk-sharing: government dollars maintain the safety net, philanthropy fuels innovation. Communicating that interdependence, with the support of granular data helps to depoliticize budget debates and rebuild the reservoir of public trust essential for sustainable human service delivery.

Climate Resilience and Sustainability

Nonprofit organizations are increasingly on the frontlines of climate-related disruptions ranging from wildfires and heatwaves to floods and infrastructure failures. As global temperatures rise and severe weather events become more frequent, the sector must grapple with both intensified service demand and the fragility of its own physical infrastructure. This section explores how climate resilience and environmental sustainability are reshaping nonprofit operations, facilities planning, and funding strategy.

Climate Impacts on Nonprofit Operations

Climate change is no longer a distant risk but a present and compounding force. Rising sea levels threaten coastal facilities; extreme heat jeopardizes the safety of vulnerable populations; and prolonged droughts increase food insecurity, pressuring food banks and emergency services. According to the U.S. Global Change Research Program (2023), nonprofit-run shelters, clinics, and community centers are disproportionately located in climate-vulnerable zones, placing both staff and service delivery at risk during environmental crises.

These disruptions drive surges in demand for heat relief programs, disaster housing, air filtration, and mobile healthcare. During the 2021 Pacific Northwest heat dome, for example, community-based nonprofits in Oregon reported a 300% spike in requests for cooling centers and hydration supplies (Climate Impact Lab, 2022). Without proactive planning, such demands can overwhelm program capacity and staff bandwidth.

Designing for Resilience

To remain operational during environmental shocks, forward-thinking nonprofits are integrating resilience into physical design, staffing models, and contingency planning. Facility retrofits, such as elevating buildings in flood-prone areas, upgrading HVAC systems, or installing solar-plus-battery microgrids are increasingly essential. These adaptations not only safeguard continuity of services, but also reduce long-term energy costs and carbon emissions.

In parallel, scenario-based emergency planning and cross-training staff for multiple roles enable organizations to pivot quickly during climate events. One Philadelphia-based food justice nonprofit now holds annual climate drills and coordinates with local mutual aid networks to pre-position supplies ahead of hurricane season. These strategies reflect a broader shift from reactive recovery to proactive preparedness.

Green Funding Mechanisms and Sustainability Commitments

Environmental sustainability also presents an emerging funding opportunity. Foundations and public agencies are ramping up investment in "green nonprofits"—organizations that either work directly on environmental issues or integrate sustainability into core operations. Green grants, resilience infrastructure funds, and ESG-aligned donor portfolios are rapidly expanding. The Inflation Reduction Act of 2022, for instance, earmarked billions in clean energy credits and facility retrofitting grants, many of which nonprofits are eligible to access (U.S. Department of Energy, 2023).

Simultaneously, funders are beginning to screen for environmental practices as part of due diligence. Nonprofits that demonstrate commitments to reducing waste, sourcing locally, and adopting low-carbon technologies are more likely to attract institutional and individual donors with climate-conscious values.

Ethics, Equity, and Climate Justice

Climate resilience must be pursued with an equity lens. Historically marginalized communities, which are often served by nonprofits, bear the brunt of environmental harm yet are least equipped to adapt. This disparity demands that sustainability initiatives not only reduce emissions but also dismantle environmental injustice. Programs that pair rooftop solar with utility bill subsidies, or community gardens with flood mitigation, exemplify solutions that are both ecological and equitable.

Leadership in this space involves modeling the values of intergenerational justice, environmental stewardship, and adaptive innovation. Strategic investments in climate resilience are not merely risk management, but moral and operational imperatives.

Regulatory Technology and Compliance Automation

As the regulatory environment for nonprofit organizations grows more complex, a new wave of tools—collectively known as regulatory technology (or "RegTech")—is transforming how compliance is achieved. Traditionally, tasks such as IRS Form 990 preparation, grant reporting, and board documentation demanded significant staff time, manual data entry, and the expertise of external consultants. Today, automation platforms powered by artificial intelligence (AI) are reshaping this administrative landscape.

From Manual Reporting to Machine Intelligence

Emerging RegTech solutions now offer dynamic workflows that auto-populate federal and foundation reports using integrated data feeds from donor databases, payroll systems, and financial software. For example, cloud-based tools like Foundation Source, Instrumentl, and GrantsEdge assist nonprofits in aligning expenditures to grant terms, reducing audit risk and improving funder relations (Tech Impact, 2023). Similarly, software suites such as Zen990 use AI to generate draft IRS Form 990s with predictive error checking and automatic flagging of anomalies.

The upside is clear: organizations can decrease staff hours spent on low-value tasks and redirect capacity toward mission delivery. A 2023 study by NTEN found that nonprofits employing AI-enhanced compliance tools reduced their annual audit preparation time by 38% while increasing reporting accuracy (NTEN, 2023). For small and mid-sized nonprofits without in-house legal or accounting departments, these tools can be especially transformative.

Implications for Governance

However, the benefits of RegTech come with governance considerations. Board members remain legally accountable for filings and disclosures, even when software automates the preparation process. This raises critical questions: Who reviews machine-generated documents? How do we validate algorithmic decisions? What safeguards ensure data integrity and privacy?

Best practices now call for a hybrid model consisting of automated preparation paired with human oversight. Boards are encouraged to establish audit or compliance subcommittees that periodically review RegTech protocols, confirm data source accuracy, and ensure that automation supports—not replaces—fiduciary diligence. Moreover, ethics guidelines should be updated to address AI bias and decision transparency, particularly when software recommends funding allocations or risk ratings.

Leaders must also anticipate future compliance trends. With federal agencies exploring blockchain-based audit trails and digital identity verification for grantees, nonprofits that proactively build technological literacy into their governance practices will be better equipped to adapt. Regulatory fluency is no longer a back-office function, but a core leadership competency in a data-driven era.

Intersection with Leadership: Guiding Nonprofits Through Uncertainty

Nonprofit leadership in the twenty-first century is defined, not by stability, but by the capacity to navigate volatility with clarity, empathy, and strategic intent. In a sector increasingly shaped by digital transformation, equity demands, regulatory complexity, and public trust erosion, effective leaders must master a blend of cognitive, emotional, and organizational competencies. This section unpacks those capacities in the context of five interlocking domains.

Systems Thinking and Adaptive Capacity

Adaptive capacity begins with systems thinking: the ability to perceive the interdependence of issues such as food insecurity, housing instability, and climate volatility. Rather than treating symptoms in isolation, adaptive leaders map connections among policy levers, funding structures, and community dynamics. Herman and Renz (2020) argue that the effectiveness of nonprofit organizations now correlates more with this adaptive responsiveness than with rigid strategic plans.

During the COVID-19 pandemic, for example, food banks that embraced cross-sector partnerships with logistics and technology firms expanded distribution volume by up to 200%—not by doing more of the same, but by reengineering how services were delivered (Feeding America, 2021).

Emotional Intelligence and Psychological Safety

Emotional intelligence (EQ) underpins every other leadership skill. Nonprofit environments often operate under high emotional labor—whether comforting clients in crisis or responding to staff burnout. Leaders with high EQ foster cultures of psychological safety in which team members feel heard, respected, and empowered to raise concerns.

A 2022 RAND study found that organizations whose CEOs delivered weekly, empathic video briefings during the pandemic retained 18% more staff than peers, underscoring the importance of transparent, emotionally attuned communication (Sontag-Padilla, Staplefoote, & Gonzalez Morgan, 2022).

Ethical Clarity and Nonpartisan Credibility

Leaders today must operate in a hyper-politicized environment in which even well-intentioned programs are subject to ideological scrutiny. Demonstrating ethical clarity and nonpartisan credibility is essential not only to sustain public funding, but to steward inclusive community trust.

Effective leaders align their programs with widely held values such as dignity, opportunity, and justice, while communicating outcomes in evidence-based, disaggregated formats. This approach fosters transparency without polarizing stakeholders and frames services as universal rights rather than ideological agendas.

Strategic Risk Taking and Innovation

High-impact nonprofit leaders do not wait for perfect conditions; rather, they create opportunity amid uncertainty. Crutchfield and Grant (2012) note that breakthrough organizations actively pursue bold initiatives at the edge of their risk tolerance, whether in the form of hybrid revenue models, cross-sector mergers, or impact investment strategies.

Board governance must evolve accordingly, shifting from risk aversion to risk intelligence by evaluating which risks are necessary to fulfill mission goals and which reflect systemic fragility. Scenario planning becomes a critical tool in this context.

Institutionalized Learning Loops

Organizations thrive, not by avoiding mistakes, but by learning from them systematically. Institutionalized learning loops embed reflection, experimentation, and course correction in program cycles and management practice. This includes after-action reviews, rapid prototyping, and investment in adaptive capacity beyond the executive tier.

Nonprofits that integrate feedback from staff, clients, and funders with real-time operational adjustments demonstrate an agility that outlasts any single leader's tenure.

Mini Case: Feeding America's Pandemic Pivot

In March 2020, as the COVID-19 pandemic shuttered schools and businesses across the U.S., food insecurity surged to unprecedented levels. Feeding America, the nation's largest domestic hunger-relief organization, faced a dual crisis: rising demand and a collapsing volunteer base, 60% of whom were retirees advised to isolate.

Rather than retreat, the organization doubled down on innovation. Partnering with technology companies and logistics firms like Amazon and Uber, Feeding America launched a national "no-contact" delivery model, rerouting surplus food from closed institutions to local distribution hubs. Data dashboards enabled real-time inventory tracking across 200 food banks.

This pivot resulted in a 200% increase in meals distributed over three months. CEO Claire Babineaux-Fontenot framed the disruption not as an emergency to survive, but as a chance to reimagine equitable food systems. Her leadership exemplified systems thinking, emotional intelligence, and adaptive risk-taking. (Source: Feeding America, 2021)

Future Trajectories: Navigating Toward 2035

As we look to the horizon of nonprofit leadership, three powerful trends are poised to redefine the sector's structure, strategy, and scope by 2035: the accelerating adoption of artificial intelligence, generational shifts in philanthropic behavior, and global innovation patterns driven by the Global South. This final section synthesizes these developments and invites readers to explore how they might reshape the nonprofit landscape over the next decade.

AI Adoption Curves and Mission Delivery

Artificial intelligence (AI) is poised to become a general-purpose technology in the nonprofit sector, on par with the internet or mobile communication. As AI applications mature, their role will expand from task automation (e.g., donor segmentation, fraud detection) to mission-centric functions such as predictive analytics for homelessness prevention or AI-assisted mental health triage.

However, adoption will occur along a staggered curve. Early adopters—primarily large institutions with robust tech capacity—are already integrating AI to streamline operations. In contrast, small and mid-sized nonprofits face steeper barriers in terms of budget, skills, and governance readiness. By 2030, we expect a bifurcation: organizations with AI-integrated workflows will exhibit markedly higher efficiency and responsiveness, while those lagging behind may struggle to meet funder and beneficiary expectations (TechSoup, 2024).

Leadership must prepare now by investing in digital fluency, ethical AI training, and partnership models that de-risk experimentation.

Demographic Transitions and Gen Z Philanthropy

Generational transition will also reconfigure funding ecosystems. By 2035, Millennials and Gen Z will comprise the majority of both nonprofit leadership and donor pools. These cohorts' philanthropic behavior differs significantly from that of their predecessors in that they value transparency, co-creation, and systems change over legacy institutions or unrestricted giving. A 2023 report by Fidelity Charitable found that 78% of Gen Z donors prefer to fund organizations aligned with their social values, often through peer-to-peer platforms or activist mutual aid channels.

Nonprofits must adapt their engagement strategies accordingly. Digital-first donor journeys, participatory grantmaking, and brand authenticity will become prerequisites for securing next-gen support. Moreover, Gen Z leaders are more likely to prioritize DEI, climate action, and mental health—driving shifts not only in what nonprofits fund, but how they govern and measure success (Council on Foundations, 2023).

The Global South Leapfrog Phenomenon

While many Global North nonprofits are encumbered by legacy systems and regulatory inertia, their counterparts in the Global South are increasingly leapfrogging traditional development models. From blockchain-based land rights verification in Kenya to SMS-based micro-philanthropy in India, these innovations bypass outdated infrastructure entirely, setting new benchmarks for cost-effective, community-led impact (World Economic Forum, 2024).

This leapfrogging is not just technological, it's epistemological. Knowledge flows are reversing as Global South organizations export methodologies, governance models, and tools to their Northern peers. Wise leaders will cultivate reciprocal learning networks and rethink the "capacity-building" paradigm in favor of global mutualism.

Scenario Exercise: Nonprofit Sector 2035

Objective: To explore how emerging trends may reshape the nonprofit sector by the year 2035, fostering systems thinking and adaptive foresight.

Instructions:

1. Divide into small teams (3–5 students).

2. Assign each group a core variable: AI adoption, Gen Z philanthropy, climate volatility, or global policy shifts.

3. Each team will construct a plausible 2035 scenario using the following prompts:

4. What does the nonprofit ecosystem look like in your scenario?

5. How have funders, beneficiaries, and workforce changed?

6. What new governance, funding, or ethical challenges have emerged?

7. What leadership capacities are most critical?

8. Prepare a 5-minute briefing with visual aids.

9. Conclude with a peer-led Q&A to stress-test assumptions.

The Path Ahead

Nonprofit leadership is no longer about maintaining the status quo—it is about preparing for what comes next. From climate shocks and digital disruption to generational change and global innovation, the terrain is shifting beneath our feet. The competencies outlined in this chapter—systems thinking, emotional intelligence, ethical clarity, strategic innovation, and adaptive learning—form the bedrock of resilient leadership.

But skills alone are not enough. Leaders must also cultivate an ethos of inquiry, humility, and courage. The future of the sector belongs to those who can navigate complexity with clarity, align values with evidence, and mobilize diverse coalitions around shared goals.

As we move through this textbook, we will translate these leadership ideals into tangible practices across budgeting, program design, fundraising, and evaluation. Your task, as a current or future nonprofit leader, is to incorporate these insights, not only into your organizational toolkit, but into your moral imagination.

Because the question is not whether the world will change, but whether we will be prepared to lead when it does.

Discussion Questions

1. Identify and describe the four major historical eras in the evolution of the U.S. nonprofit sector. How did each era influence current governance practices?

2. How do nonprofit organizations contribute to both the U.S. economy and civil society? Cite key statistics.

3. Compare the characteristics of nonprofit organizations to those of for-profit and public sector entities.

4. What are the major leadership competencies required in today's nonprofit sector?

5. Explain the importance of DEI in nonprofit governance and program delivery. Provide current examples.

6. How can artificial intelligence and digital tools enhance or challenge nonprofit operations?

7. Reflect on your own organization or one you admire. Where does it fall on the organizational lifecycle curve?

Field Markers

1. **Adaptive Capacity:** The ability of an organization to adjust its strategies and operations in response to external changes or challenges.

2. **DEI (Diversity, Equity, and Inclusion):** A framework that promotes fair treatment, access, and opportunity for all individuals while eliminating barriers to participation and advancement.

3. **Emotional Intelligence:** The capacity to recognize, understand, and manage one's own emotions and the emotions of others.

4. **Lifecycle Curve:** A conceptual model outlining the various

stages of organizational development: startup, growth, maturity, and turnaround/closure.

5. **Mission Centricity:** A focus on achieving and aligning all organizational activities with a clearly defined mission or public purpose.

6. **Regulatory Technology (RegTech):** Software tools that assist organizations in complying with regulatory requirements through automation and data management.

7. **Social Return on Investment (SROI):** A framework for measuring and accounting for the broader social, economic, and environmental value generated by an organization's activities.

- Chapter 2 -

Budget Development

Budget development is one of the most consequential responsibilities entrusted to nonprofit leaders. A well-constructed budget is not simply an administrative requirement—it is a strategic document that demonstrates mission priorities, guides decision-making, and reflects organizational values. This chapter positions budgeting as a core leadership competency, emphasizing that effective resource planning is both a technical discipline and a moral imperative.

Unlike budgets in the for-profit sector, where success is measured by profitability, nonprofit budgets are evaluated in terms of how effectively financial resources are deployed to achieve public benefit. This unique standard requires leaders to balance financial stewardship with mission alignment, anticipate uncertainties, and communicate transparently with stakeholders across sectors.

Learning Objectives

By the end of Chapter 2, readers will be able to:

1. Identify the essential components and construction methods of nonprofit budgets, including distinctions from for-profit financial planning.

2. Align budgeting practices with strategic objectives to ensure that resource allocation advances mission effectiveness and organizational sustainability.

3. Construct multi-year budgets and apply forecasting techniques to support long-term planning, risk mitigation, and capacity growth.

4. Employ scenario planning methodologies to anticipate funding disruptions and proactively design financial contingency strategies.

5. Develop transparent, audience-specific approaches to communicating financial health using tools such as dashboards, KPIs, and financial reports.

6. Apply the principles of financial storytelling to translate numerical data into mission-driven narratives that strengthen donor confidence and stakeholder engagement.

Quick-Glance Map of Chapter 2

Section	Learning Objectives
The Basics of Budgeting	Understand core components and budgeting methodologies unique to the nonprofit sector.
Budget-Strategy Alignment	Align financial plans with organizational goals and performance metrics.
Multi-Year Budgeting	Build resilient, forward-looking budgets that support sustainability and growth.
Scenario Planning	Prepare for uncertainty through structured, risk-informed financial modeling.
Communicating Financial Health	Translate complex financial data into accessible reports and dashboards for diverse audiences.
Financial Storytelling	Leverage budgets as narrative tools that demonstrate impact and inspire stakeholder engagement.

The Basics of Budgeting for Nonprofits

A nonprofit budget is more than a ledger of income and expenditures—it is a leadership tool that defines how values are operationalized through fiscal decisions. As the financial blueprint of the organization, the budget directs resources toward mission fulfillment, enables strategic planning, and signals accountability to internal and external stakeholders.

Unlike corporate budgets, which are driven by profit maximization, nonprofit budgets are designed to optimize impact within resource constraints (National Council of Nonprofits, 2023). This fundamental difference requires leaders to understand not only the mechanics of budgeting but also the ethical considerations inherent in allocating limited funds across competing priorities.

Core Budget Components

At a minimum, every nonprofit budget includes two primary categories: revenue and expenses.

Revenue sources, which may be restricted, typically include:

1. Foundation and government grants

2. Individual and corporate donations

3. Membership dues

4. Earned income (e.g., ticket sales, program fees)

5. Government contracts and fee-for-service arrangements

Expenses are commonly divided into:

Programmatic costs, which directly support service delivery

(e.g., educational materials, food distribution, clinical staff salaries)

Administrative expenses, including management, office infrastructure, compliance, and technology

Fundraising costs, which encompass development staff, donor stewardship, campaigns, and grant writing

Restricted grants and donations are financial contributions that carry legally binding stipulations regarding their use, as defined by the donating entity or person. These funds must be allocated strictly for the purposes outlined in the original agreement, the grant award letter or the donor's stated intention. Misuse or misallocation of restricted funds, such as applying them to unrelated programs or overhead, can constitute a breach of fiduciary duty. This may trigger legal, reputational, or financial consequences, including funder sanctions or loss of public trust (National Council of Nonprofits, 2023).

Zero-based Budgeting

Zero-based budgeting (ZBB) is a rigorous financial planning methodology that requires each budget item to be justified from scratch during each planning cycle, rather than being based on historical expenditures. This approach promotes strategic alignment by ensuring that all allocations reflect current organizational priorities, rather than legacy practices. While ZBB can be resource-intensive, especially for smaller nonprofits, it enhances fiscal discipline, fosters critical review of spending assumptions, and can uncover inefficiencies that incremental budgeting may obscure (Millesen & Carman, 2022).

Finally, nonprofit budgets must comply with a complex array of fiscal accountability standards. These include the requirements set forth by funding agencies, Internal Revenue Service Form 990 reporting obligations for tax-exempt organizations, and state-level nonprofit accounting statutes. Adhering to these standards is not merely procedural—it is essential for sustaining public confidence, maintaining good standing with regulators, and preserving the organization's ability to secure future funding (IRS, 2023). Meticulous compliance with these frameworks reflects a commitment to transparency and stewardship, both of which are central to ethical nonprofit leadership.

Budgeting Methodologies

Nonprofit leaders may choose among the several approaches to budget construction mentioned above, each having its own strategic implications:

6. **Incremental Budgeting:** Builds on prior-year figures with modest adjustments. This method is efficient for stable organizations but risks perpetuating outdated assumptions or inefficiencies.

7. **Zero-Based Budgeting (ZBB):** Requires each line item to be justified annually from the ground up. While labor-intensive, ZBB promotes alignment with current priorities and encourages financial discipline.

8. **Activity-Based Budgeting (ABB):** Connects financial planning directly to specific programs or services. ABB is especially useful for organizations undergoing programmatic restructuring or preparing grant budgets tied to outcomes.

9. **Flexible or Contingency Budgets:** Include adjustable components based on revenue performance or operational conditions. These models enhance organizational agility and are particularly relevant in uncertain funding environments.

Steps in Budget Development

The budgeting process typically follows these sequential phases:

1. **Historical and Trend Analysis:** Review of prior financial performance, including seasonal variations, one-time events, and multi-year trends.

2. **Stakeholder Engagement:** Input from program managers, finance staff, and board committees ensures accuracy and buy-in.

3. **Regulatory and Compliance Review:** Budgets must adhere to funder requirements, IRS Form 990 standards, and state-level nonprofit accounting rules.

4. **Drafting and Internal Vetting:** The finance team drafts the preliminary budget, which is then iteratively reviewed with senior leadership.

5. **Board Review and Approval:** Final approval is granted by the board of directors, typically upon recommendation of a finance or executive committee.

6. **Implementation and Monitoring:** Budgets must be tracked against actuals, with quarterly variance analyses and mid-year adjustments as needed.

Common Pitfalls and Leadership Challenges

Nonprofit leaders must avoid several recurring budgeting errors:

1. **Underestimating Overhead:** Artificially minimizing administrative or fundraising costs to satisfy external expectations can impair organizational effectiveness.

2. **Overdependence on One-Time Funding:** Relying on event-based income or single-year grants without a diversifi-

cation strategy introduces instability.

3. **Inadequate Cash Flow Planning:** Budgets that appear balanced on paper may conceal liquidity gaps, particularly when funding is disbursed quarterly or reimbursed post-service.

Leadership must set a tone of transparency and realism, fostering an environment in which budget assumptions are challenged constructively and aligned with strategic goals.

Technology Tools and Transparency Practices

Modern budgeting tools such as QuickBooks Online, Aplos, or Sage Intacct support efficient budget development and reporting. These platforms allow for integration with donor databases, payroll systems, and audit workflows. Importantly, they also support dashboard-based transparency, which is an increasingly common expectation among funders and community stakeholders.

Publishing summary budgets in annual reports, presenting program cost breakdowns in donor communications, and training staff in budget literacy are all leadership practices that build trust and operational resilience.

Budgeting is not a finance team task—it is a leadership responsibility that demands strategic foresight, ethical clarity, and stakeholder alignment. Mastery of budgeting fundamentals enables nonprofit professionals to steward resources with integrity, navigate uncertainty with confidence, and advance the mission with fiscal credibility.

Aligning Budgets with Strategic Goals

An effective nonprofit budget reflects organizational purpose in financial form. Strategic alignment between budgeting and mission ensures that every dollar spent moves the organization closer to its intended outcomes. This section focuses on the ways in which nonprofit leaders embed strategy in budgeting decisions, ensuring allocation of fiscal resources in ways that are intentional, impactful, and responsive to evolving priorities.

The use of logic models and impact-based budgeting aligns with best practices in both public and nonprofit strategic planning (Bryson, 2021).

The Budget as a Strategic Tool

In mission-driven organizations, the budget serves as a tactical expression of the strategic plan. Rather than functioning as a static financial document, the budget should dynamically allocate resources in alignment with the organization's theory of change, program goals, and operational priorities.

For example, if an environmental nonprofit's strategic plan includes expansion of youth education programs in underserved communities, the budget must reflect investment in outreach staff, curriculum development, transportation, and possibly language access services. A budget that does not implement these strategic intents is disconnected from mission effectiveness, regardless of how balanced it may appear.

Strategic budgeting demands proactive decision-making: which programs to expand, which to sunset, and where to invest in infrastructure to support long-term sustainability. Leaders must assess not only direct program costs, but also capacity-building needs such as staff development, data systems, and partnership cultivation.

Tactical Budgeting Frameworks

To ensure alignment between strategy and budgeting, nonprofit leaders often employ the following tools and frameworks:

Logic Models: Visually link inputs (budget), activities, outputs, and outcomes. Logic models help boards and funders see the intended impact of financial allocations.

Cost Centers: Assign budget lines to specific departments or programs. This allows leaders to evaluate whether spending is proportionate to strategic importance and performance outcomes.

Outcomes-Based Budgeting (OBB): Allocates resources according to expected results, such as "cost per graduate" or "cost per family housed," rather than historical line items alone. This is typically provided in a dashboard format during the reporting process.

Balanced Scorecards: Integrate financial, operational, and impact metrics into a unified tracking system. This tool supports mid-year course corrections and board-level oversight.

Governance and Leadership Alignment

Board oversight plays a central role in budget-strategy alignment. The finance committee should assess whether proposed budgets are grounded in the strategic plan, supported by data, and risk-adjusted for financial sustainability. Regular joint meetings between board finance and program committees can foster cross-functional understanding and prevent mission drift.

Executive directors and senior staff are responsible for ensuring that budget decisions are informed by frontline realities. Engaging program leaders in the budgeting process help to validate assumptions and uncover operational blind spots. This participatory approach builds internal alignment and strengthens accountability.

Leaders should also consider timing: aligning the annual budgeting cycle with strategic planning reviews ensures that financial plans are consistently tied to evolving goals rather than outdated frameworks.

Red Flags that Indicate Misalignment

Red flags that signal misalignment between a nonprofit's budget and its strategic goals often emerge incrementally, making them easy to overlook without intentional scrutiny.

A primary indicator of such misalignment emerges when programs receive disproportionate funding relative to their strategic value or demonstrated outcomes. For instance, legacy programs may continue to command significant budget allocations due to historical precedent or internal politics, even as newer initiatives that align more directly with current strategic objectives remain underfunded. This imbalance can distort organizational priorities, dilute impact, and erode mission coherence.

Another subtle warning sign appears when budget surpluses accumulate, not because of prudent financial management, but due to chronic underinvestment in areas central to the mission. Although maintaining reserves is essential for fiscal stability, consistent underspending in critical programmatic domains may indicate a lack of strategic vision or risk aversion. In such cases, the surplus reflects missed opportunities rather than operational efficiency and may point to internal barriers, such as fear of innovation or inadequate planning capacity, that constrain the organization's ability to scale its impact.

Underfunding core infrastructure, including technology systems, performance evaluation, and staff development, is also a common and consequential form of misalignment. These foundational elements are often treated as overhead or even as a luxury, and therefore are often not prioritized in budgeting discussions, despite their critical role in enabling long-term effectiveness and sustainability. When such investments are repeatedly deferred, the organization may struggle to measure outcomes, manage growth, or respond to emerging challenges, thus undermining its overall strategic agility.

Finally, a budget that fails to account for known external variables, such as anticipated policy changes, shifts in donor behavior, or the expiration of major grants, demonstrates a reactive rather than proactive approach to financial planning. Strategic budgeting requires not only alignment with internal goals but also responsiveness to the external landscape. Overlooking foreseeable disruptions places the organization at risk of abrupt funding shortfalls, program interruptions, or reputational damage due to a perceived lack of preparation.

Addressing these forms of misalignment demands honest reflection, active stakeholder engagement, and a willingness to reallocate resources, even when such changes are politically sensitive or institutionally uncomfortable. Strategic budgeting is not a passive accounting function but a dynamic leadership discipline. By rigorously linking financial decisions to mission priorities, nonprofit leaders foster transparency, enhance organizational performance, and strengthen stakeholder trust. A well-aligned budget does more than document financial intent, it embodies a commitment to purposeful action, transforming vision into measurable impact.

Multi-Year Budgeting for Sustainability

While annual budgets offer a snapshot of financial health, they often fall short of supporting long-term organizational growth and resilience. Multi-year budgeting (typically spanning three to five years) is a forward-looking approach that helps to align fiscal planning with strategic vision. This approach allows nonprofit leaders to anticipate change, manage risk, and sequence investments in a sustainable manner.

Reserves, ideally 5–10% of annual operating revenue, are critical for organizational agility and risk mitigation (National Council of Nonprofits, 2023). Organizations using multi-year budgets were 40% more likely to hit growth targets, largely because they could anticipate challenges like donor attrition or rising supply costs (Nonprofit Finance Fund, 2022). This approach complements strategic planning frameworks that emphasize foresight and scenario modeling (Bryson, 2021).

Why Multi-Year Budgeting Matters

Nonprofits operate in environments marked by funding volatility, shifting policy landscapes, and evolving community needs. Single-year budgets may enable compliance and short-term planning, but they often obscure structural weaknesses or underfunded priorities. A multi-year budget, by contrast, serves as both a financial roadmap and a strategic alignment tool.

Multi-year frameworks allow leaders to:

1. Forecast revenue diversification efforts

2. Phase in programmatic expansions or capital improvements

3. Evaluate long-term cost structures

4. Strategically build and replenish reserves

5. Sustainably model staffing and compensation plans

Consider a workforce development nonprofit seeking to launch a new job training initiative. A three-year budget might allocate Year 1 to curriculum development and pilot testing, Year 2 to staff recruitment and program scaling, and Year 3 to full implementation and impact measurement. This phased planning ensures that investment aligns with operational readiness and anticipated outcomes.

Core Components of a Multi-Year Budget

Revenue Forecasting

1. Blends historical trends with forward-looking projections for each funding source (e.g., foundation grants, fee-for-service income).

2. Applies conservative assumptions to mitigate optimism bias.

3. Incorporates potential shifts in donor behavior, public funding priorities, or economic conditions.

Expense Planning

1. Factors in inflation, cost-of-living adjustments, and capital asset maintenance.

2. Includes strategic investments, such as new technology, data infrastructure, or staff development.

3. Plans for contingencies such as insurance rate increases or regulatory compliance costs.

4. Capital and Infrastructure Planning (include separate project budgets to call these out)

5. Identifies long-term facility needs, equipment upgrades, or reserve targets.

6. Model depreciation, major repairs, and financing options over time.

Contingency and Reserves

1. Best practice recommends reserving 5–10% of annual operating revenue.
2. Reserves may be restricted for items such as capital improvements or unrestricted for general stabilization.

Leadership Practices and Governance Implications

Multi-year budgeting requires active engagement from the board of directors, particularly from its finance and audit committees. Board members must understand the assumptions embedded in forecasts and be prepared to challenge unrealistic expectations. Scenario testing (asking "what if" questions) builds a culture of fiscal agility and shared accountability.

Executive leadership plays a pivotal role in bridging finance and strategy. By involving program directors and senior staff in the multi-year budgeting process, leaders ensure that budget plans reflect both strategic aspirations and operational constraints. Internal alignment is especially crucial when long-term projections involve fundraising capacity building, program scaling, or staff expansion.

The Role of Rolling Forecasts

Many nonprofits complement multi-year budgets with rolling forecasts—dynamic updates to financial projections that incorporate new information quarterly or biannually. This adaptive approach allows for responsive recalibration based on real-time performance and external developments.

For instance, a nonprofit experiencing a delay in a major grant disbursement might revise staffing projections and shift discretionary expenditures into the next fiscal year. This level of agility is increasingly vital in an era of economic uncertainty and rapid policy change.

Technology Tools

Software solutions such as Adaptive Insights, Vena, or Questica provide modeling capabilities that support multi-year forecasting. These platforms allow organizations to visualize the downstream impacts of financial decisions, such as a salary increase or a facilities lease across multiple budget cycles.

Built-in scenario planning features help compare best-case, base-case, and worst-case financial positions, offering a strategic edge in board presentations and funder negotiations.

Benefits and Risks

Benefits:

3. Clarifies funding gaps and timing mismatches.

4. Enhances credibility with funders and institutional partners.

5. Improves resource sequencing and investment pacing.

6. Strengthens organizational sustainability and mission delivery.

Risks:

7. Assumes long-range predictability that may not exist.

8. Requires significant data accuracy and financial literacy.

9. May lead to rigidity if not coupled with adaptive planning tools.

Multi-year budgeting shifts the focus from tactical survival to strategic stewardship. It enables nonprofit leaders to manage uncertainty, invest wisely, and communicate long-term vision with confidence. By institutionalizing this discipline, organizations become better equipped to sustain impact, adapt to change, and earn the trust of stakeholders whose support extends well beyond a single fiscal year.

Scenario Planning for Financial Uncertainty

In a rapidly changing funding and policy environment, nonprofit organizations must move beyond reactive budgeting. Scenario planning offers a proactive financial strategy that equips organizations to model uncertainty, anticipate risk, and adapt resource allocation in response to both internal fluctuations and external disruptions. This discipline is increasingly recognized as an essential component of financial resilience and strategic leadership in the nonprofit sector.

What Is Scenario Planning?

Scenario planning is the process of envisioning multiple plausible financial futures and preparing responsive strategies for each. Rather than attempting to predict a single outcome, organizations explore a range of potential scenarios—such as loss of major funding, policy changes, demand spikes, or economic downturns—and model how each would affect operations, liquidity, and impact delivery (National Council of Nonprofits, 2023).

A well-structured scenario planning exercise typically includes:

10. **Identifying Critical Variables:** Revenue concentration, fixed vs. variable costs, donor dependencies, inflation, and policy volatility.

11. **Developing Scenarios:** Best-case, moderate, and worst-case financial projections.

12. **Building Response Plans:** Budget triggers, spending freezes, reserve deployment strategies, staffing adjustments, or program scaling.

13. **Reviewing and Revising Regularly:** Keeping scenarios current with new data and evolving perspectives.

This approach was widely adopted during the COVID-19 pandemic, when organizations experienced unprecedented disruptions to both funding streams and service models. Nonprofits with existing scenario plans were able to act swiftly by activating contingency measures, securing bridge funding, or pivoting to virtual delivery channels (Nonprofit Finance Fund, 2022).

Integrating Scenario Planning into Budget Development

Scenario planning should be embedded in the budgeting cycle not treated as an isolated activity. Leaders should incorporate risk-based thinking into annual budget deliberations, especially when developing multi-year forecasts or strategic growth initiatives.

Practical tools include:

14. **Rolling Forecasts:** Dynamic updates that adjust core budget assumptions on a quarterly or biannual basis.

15. **Decision Thresholds:** Predetermined financial indicators that trigger response protocols (e.g., initiating cost controls if revenue drops by 15% for two consecutive quarters).

16. **Stress Testing:** Simulating how current operations would fare under varied economic conditions.

For example, a youth development nonprofit might model the impact of losing a government contract by analyzing which programs would require cuts, what reserves could be deployed, and how communications with stakeholders would be managed.

Technology Tools and Dashboards

Modern budgeting software, such as Adaptive Insights, Vena Solutions, or Questica, enables real-time scenario modeling by automating cash flow forecasting, sensitivity analysis, and funding simulations. These tools allow finance teams to adjust variables such as donor retention rates, inflation factors, or staffing costs and immediately visualize their downstream effects (Bryson, 2021).

Visualization tools can also support governance. Boards are more likely to engage meaningfully with scenario planning when presented with intuitive dashboards rather than dense spreadsheets. Dashboards showing the financial impact of different scenarios reinforce fiduciary responsibility and strategic decision-making.

Organizational Culture and Leadership Considerations

One barrier to effective scenario planning is cultural: some boards and staff resist "negative" modeling, fearing that it signals pessimism or weakens donor confidence. However, evidence suggests the opposite. Transparent planning for volatility increases stakeholder trust, strengthens board oversight, and can improve donor retention by reinforcing an organization's maturity and readiness (National Council of Nonprofits, 2023).

Leadership must normalize uncertainty as a management constant, rather than perceiving it as an anomaly. Executive teams that facilitate inclusive scenario planning processes and draw insights from finance, programs, fundraising, and operations are better equipped to detect blind spots and make equitable, informed decisions.

Case Example: COVID-19 and Theater Resilience

During the early months of the COVID-19 pandemic, a regional theater company in the Pacific Northwest activated a previously modeled scenario for performance cancellations. The scenario included negotiated rent deferrals, a pivot to virtual performances, and a tiered furlough plan. As a result, the theater retained 80% of its operating revenue and avoided permanent layoffs, demonstrating the impact of proactive financial foresight (Nonprofit Finance Fund, 2022).

Scenario planning transforms financial management from a reactive task into a leadership strategy. It enables nonprofits to frame uncertainty not as a threat, but as a navigable variable within an informed, adaptive framework. As economic, political, and environmental disruptions become more frequent, scenario planning will continue to distinguish resilient, high-performing nonprofit organizations from those that are chronically unprepared.

Communicating Financial Health to Stakeholders

Transparent financial communication is a hallmark of ethical leadership and is a crucial mechanism for building trust across stakeholder groups. For nonprofit organizations, communicating financial health is not merely a reporting function—it is a strategic imperative that reinforces accountability, informs decision-making, and strengthens public confidence. During an era in which public scrutiny is high and funding landscapes are complex, nonprofit leaders must elevate how financial information is shared, interpreted, and contextualized.

The Imperative of Radical Accountability

In Chapter One, the concept of radical accountability was introduced as a leadership philosophy that is grounded in transparency, ethical stewardship, and proactive disclosure. In the financial context, radical accountability requires nonprofit leaders to go beyond basic compliance to actively communicate both fiscal strengths and vulnerabilities in clear, accessible terms. This includes:

- Publicly sharing operating budgets and audited financials.
- Explaining budget-to-actual variances in language understandable to non-financial audiences.
- Framing financial decisions in terms of mission impact and equity considerations.
- Acknowledging financial risks and the ways in which these risks are being mitigated.

Rather than guarding financial data as privileged information, leaders committed to radical accountability position financial health as a shared concern. In doing so, they invite dialogue, demonstrate responsibility, and model trustworthiness.

Financial Reports:
The Foundation of Transparency

Standard financial reports remain essential tools for communicating fiscal position and performance:

- **Statement of Financial Position (Balance Sheet):** Summarizes assets, liabilities, and net assets.
- **Statement of Activities (Income Statement):** Tracks revenues and expenses over a reporting period.
- **Statement of Cash Flows:** Details how cash moves through operations, investing, and financing activities.
- **IRS Form 990:** A public document that includes revenue, expenses, compensation, and program details.

These reports, except the 990, which is annual, should be produced at least quarterly and made accessible to internal leadership and board members. Whereever feasible, high-level summaries should also be shared with external stakeholders via annual reports, websites, and donor updates (IRS, 2023).

Although these documents satisfy regulatory requirements, they are rarely effective communication tools for most non-financial audiences. Because of this deficiency, it is recommended that financial statements be augmented using financial dashboards.

Dashboards: Enhancing Understanding and Engagement

Financial dashboards translate complex datasets into visual, intuitive formats that highlight key performance indicators (KPIs). When well-designed, dashboards promote financial literacy and enable real-time engagement by board members, staff, and funders alike.

Effective dashboards typically include:

- Program efficiency ratios (program vs. admin costs)
- Cash runway (months of operational cash on hand)
- Donor retention rates
- Grant utilization rates
- Budget vs. actuals by department or program

Reserve balance trends

Tools such as Power BI, Tableau, and Google Data Studio offer flexible platforms for customizing dashboards to meet various stakeholder needs. For example, a development team may track donor acquisition costs, while the executive team monitors liquidity and earned revenue diversification.

Dashboards also play a critical role in real-time decision-making.

By visualizing trends over time, they enable leadership to identify variances early and take corrective action before issues escalate.

Tailoring Financial Communication by Audience

Not all stakeholders require the same level of detail or analysis. An effective communication strategy differentiates by audience:

- Board members need strategic summaries, forecasts, and risk indicators.
- Staff benefit from understanding the ways in which budget priorities affect program execution.
- Funders and donors want to see efficiency, impact, and sustainability.
- Community stakeholders are best served by simplified narratives that demonstrate how financial resources benefit the public good.

Using plain language (e.g., "emergency reserves" instead of "unrestricted net assets") enhances accessibility. Visual tools such as infographics, dashboards, and data snapshots allow organizations to move from disclosure to storytelling.

Case Example: Dashboard-Driven Donor Confidence

A regional food bank implemented a public-facing dashboard tracking cost per meal, monthly donation trends, and impact metrics such as households served. During a year of rising food costs, the organization used this dashboard to transparently communicate budget pressures, highlight operational efficiencies, and request specific donor support. The result: a 22% increase in year-end donations, with 84% of recurring donors citing "clarity of financial need" as a reason for renewing support (Nonprofit Tech for Good, 2022).

Communicating financial health goes far beyond generating reports: its essence consists of telling the truth with clarity, precision, and purpose. Leaders who embrace radical accountability not only meet disclosure requirements but build lasting trust. When financial transparency is paired with compelling visuals and contextual storytelling, organizations transform numbers into meaning, and stakeholders into champions of the mission.

Financial Storytelling: Using Budgets to Reinforce Mission Narratives

For nonprofit leaders, financial reports and budgets are not just compliance tools, they represent crucial opportunities to shape perception, mobilize support, and demonstrate impact. Financial storytelling is the discipline of translating budget data into compelling, mission-centered narratives that resonate with funders, partners, and the public. When executed effectively, this approach connects the "what" of the budget to the "why" of the organization, reinforcing transparency, accountability, and community trust.

The Purpose of Financial Storytelling

At its core, financial storytelling answers two fundamental questions:

- How does every dollar advance our mission?
- Why should stakeholders care about our budget decisions?

These narratives link numbers to real-world outcomes, transforming line items into lived experiences. Viewed in the context of radical accountability, financial storytelling is not about marketing spin; rather it is about truthfully and clearly showing the ways in which fiscal stewardship drives change.

Key Elements of Effective Financial Storytelling

Contextualization

Budgets and financial statements must be framed in terms of meaning. For example, rather than stating a $50,000 allocation to food distribution, a nonprofit might explain, "This funding will provide 60,000 meals to 2,500 families over the winter months."

Humanization

Effective storytelling introduces voices and experiences. Highlighting a beneficiary, staff member, or community partner illustrates the human impact of financial decisions. For instance: "Maria, a community nurse, uses our mobile clinic, funded through unrestricted reserves, to reach 1,200 rural patients annually."

Visualization

Infographics, short videos, and data dashboards make abstract data accessible. A simple bar chart showing budget growth alongside service expansion or an impact map tracking regional reach can convey progress better than tables of numbers.

Balance

Transparency means telling the full story, including constraints, tradeoffs, and setbacks. For example, a theater company facing a 20% venue rental increase might explain how shifting to outdoor performances reduced costs and increased access for underrepresented audiences.

Social Return on Investment (SROI)

A powerful framework for financial storytelling is Social Return on Investment (SROI), which quantifies the social, environmental, and economic value created by nonprofit programs. SROI goes beyond financial metrics to assess how resources contribute to positive societal change.

An SROI of 3:1 means that for every $1 invested, the organization creates $3 in measurable social value.

Example:

A reentry program for formerly incarcerated individuals tracks reduced recidivism, increased employment, and improved mental health among participants. Based on external benchmarks, such as cost savings from avoided incarceration, the program calculates that $500,000 in funding produces $1.6 million in community savings, an SROI of 3.2:1.

This type of analysis can be shared with grantmakers, donors, and policymakers to demonstrate effectiveness, inform funding decisions, and shape public perception.

Caution: SROI calculations require rigor. Avoid inflated estimates or casual claims. Use validated data sources and clearly explain assumptions.

Case Study 1: Housing First Coalition

Challenge: A coalition of nonprofits providing permanent supportive housing needed to justify continued investment from city council members.

Approach: Using financial storytelling, they linked budget lines to specific client outcomes of reduced emergency department visits, increased housing stability, and employment gains. Their dashboard showed that each $10,000 investment prevented an average of three costly shelter nights and two ED visits annually.

Result: The narrative shifted the conversation from "housing cost" to "health system savings and human dignity," leading to a 15% increase in municipal funding.

Case Study 2: Rural Literacy Initiative

Challenge: A rural education nonprofit struggled to maintain donor interest in long-term programming.

Approach: They redesigned their annual report to include infographics that demonstrated reading gains per dollar invested, shared student testimonials, and published an SROI estimate based on improved graduation rates and future income projections.

Result: Individual donor retention increased 27% year-over-year. A regional foundation also doubled its unrestricted support.

Best Practices for Leaders

- Train program staff to collect qualitative and quantitative data that support storytelling.
- Use storytelling in grant proposals, annual reports, and board presentations.
- Pair budget presentations with mission narratives at board and donor meetings.
- Use consistent themes and formats across platforms (e.g., "Impact per Dollar" series on social media).

Financial storytelling is not embellishment—it is clarity in service of mission. By grounding budgets in human outcomes and aligning financial decisions with social impact, nonprofit leaders elevate financial reporting from obligation to opportunity. In a sector where credibility and connection are everything, the ability to communicate the why behind the numbers is a defining leadership skill.

Chapter Summary

Chapter 2 explored the essential leadership responsibility of nonprofit budget development. Beginning with foundational principles, it outlined how to construct a compliant, mission-aligned budget and progressed to advanced strategies such as multi-year forecasting, scenario planning, financial communication, and storytelling. The chapter emphasized that budgeting is not a purely technical task, but is a strategic, ethical, and communicative process that links financial resources to organizational impact. Through exercises, tools, and real-world examples, readers learned to steward financial data as a means of accountability, engagement, and vision execution.

Discussion Questions

1. What are the core components of a nonprofit budget, and how do these differ from for-profit budgeting structures?

2. How can nonprofit leaders ensure that their budgets align with strategic goals and mission outcomes?

3. Describe the advantages of multi-year budgeting and provide an example of when this approach is essential.

4. What is scenario planning, and how can it enhance organizational resilience?

5. How can dashboards be used to communicate financial health to different stakeholder groups?

6. Define Social Return on Investment (SROI) and explain how it can be used in financial storytelling.

7. What does radical accountability look like in financial practice, and why is it important for nonprofit leadership?

Field Markers

Cash Runway: The number of months an organization can operate with current unrestricted cash reserves.

Dashboard: A visual tool for displaying real-time performance metrics to aid decision-making and promote transparency.

Multi-Year Budgeting: A financial planning process that spans multiple fiscal years, typically 3–5, to support long-term strategy and sustainability.

Outcome-Based Budgeting (OBB): A budgeting method that allocates resources based on desired outcomes or impacts, rather than historical expenditures.

Radical Accountability: A leadership approach that prioritizes extreme transparency, ethical clarity, and proactive financial communication.

Scenario Planning: The process of modeling multiple financial futures and designing strategic responses to potential risks.

Social Return on Investment (SROI): A framework for evaluating the social, environmental, or economic value created for every dollar invested.

Restricted Funds: Donor-designated resources that can only be used for specific purposes, as outlined in funding agreements.

Zero-Based Budgeting (ZBB): A budgeting approach in which all expenses must be justified each year, regardless of previous budgets.

– Chapter 3 –

Innovative Fundraising Strategies

Fundraising is not simply a functional task, rather it is a core leadership responsibility in the nonprofit sector. Successful fundraising does not rely solely on tactics. Whether one is writing a foundation proposal, launching an online appeal, or building long-term donor relationships, fundraising demands thoughtful planning, principled choices, and a genuine commitment to connection. Trust, transparency, and consistency—not just persuasion—are what ultimately sustain the process.

This chapter explores a range of fundraising strategies ranging from time-tested methods such as grant writing to emerging tools in digital fundraising. It highlights the critical role of nonprofit leaders in ensuring that revenue generation remains aligned with the organization's mission, values, and commitment to equity. Readers will find practical guidance in writing persuasive appeals, forming meaningful partnerships with businesses, and maintaining donor engagement through thoughtful stewardship.

Leaders will also explore how to create a culture of philanthropy that extends across staff and board, and how to assess the social return on investment (SROI) of their efforts. In today's competitive philanthropic environment, successful organizations are not only chasing money, but are building authentic, sustained relationships rooted in trust, impact, and shared values.

Learning Objectives

By the end of Chapter 3, readers will be able to:

1. Explain the strategic and ethical foundations of fundraising in the nonprofit sector and describe its evolution.

2. Develop competitive, mission-aligned grant proposals that reflect funder priorities, organizational capacity, and long-term sustainability.

3. Design and implement donor engagement strategies that cultivate trust, align with donor motivations, and support long-term retention.

4. Construct inclusive, community-based fundraising campaigns that reflect grassroots values and expand philanthropic participation.

5. Utilize digital tools and platforms, including crowdfunding, peer-to-peer fundraising, and social media, to broaden donor outreach and increase giving.

6. Evaluate and structure corporate partnerships that balance revenue generation with mission integrity and ethical brand alignment.

7. Strengthen donor retention through intentional stewardship, impactful communication, and relational fundraising practices.

8. Employ micro-philanthropy techniques to engage small-dollar donors and build equitable, broad-based donor communities.

9. Integrate equity and justice into fundraising strategy by identifying and mitigating power imbalances, centering

community voice, and adopting inclusive practices.

10. Cultivate a culture of philanthropy that engages staff, board, and community as collaborative stewards of mission and financial health.

11. Assess the potential of social enterprise and fee-for-service models as complementary revenue strategies that reinforce mission goals.

Quick-Glance Map of Chapter 3: Innovative Fundraising Strategies

Section	Learning Objectives
Introduction to Fundraising	Understand the strategic, ethical, and historical foundations of nonprofit fundraising.
Grant Writing Essentials	Learn how to craft competitive proposals and build long-term funder relationships.
Engaging Donors	Explore techniques to effectively cultivate, solicit, and steward individual donors.
Community-Based Fundraising	Design inclusive campaigns that leverage local participation and grassroots energy.
Digital Fundraising	Apply social media, peer-to-peer tools, and crowdfunding to broaden the donor base.
Corporate Partnerships	Structure ethical, mission-aligned sponsorships and CSR collaborations.

Section	Learning Objectives
Donor Retention	Strengthen donor loyalty through consistent stewardship and effective communication.
Micro-Philanthropy	Engage small-dollar donors at scale with monthly giving and low-barrier appeals.
Equity and Power in Fundraising	Challenge traditional models and adopt community-centered, justice-based strategies.
Culture of Philanthropy	Build an internal culture where everyone contributes to sustainable fundraising.
Social Enterprise	Launch earned-income ventures that align with the mission and expand sustainability.
Fee-for-Service Models	Implement government and private payor reimbursement models with strategic oversight.

Introduction to Fundraising in the Nonprofit Sector

Fundraising is more than a revenue-generating function: it is a central expression of nonprofit leadership, strategy, and values. In a sector defined by public benefit rather than private gain, fundraising links mission to means. Nonprofit leaders must understand fundraising, not simply as a financial survival tool, but as a relational and ethical practice that sustains community trust and organizational credibility (Tempel, Seiler, & Burlingame, 2016).

Unlike sales in the for-profit sector, which rely on transactional exchange, fundraising depends on shared purpose and long-term engagement. Donors do not receive tangible goods or services in return for their contributions; instead, they invest in the promise of social impact. It is the responsibility of nonprofit leaders to demonstrate that this promise is being fulfilled (Breeze, 2017).

The Strategic Role of Fundraising

Fundraising is a leadership competency that intersects with every organizational function—from program design to governance, financial management to communications. A robust fundraising strategy must be integrated with strategic planning, guided by data, and aligned with the organization's core values (Burnett, 2021).

Strategic fundraising answers critical questions:

- Which funding sources best align with our mission and values?
- What mix of short-term and long-term revenue streams will ensure sustainability?
- How do we communicate our impact to inspire trust and action?

An effective fundraising strategy is diversified and intentional. Over-reliance on a single source, such as a government grant or annual gala, exposes the organization to unnecessary risk. Leaders must develop a resilient funding portfolio that includes institutional grants, individual donations, earned income, and partnerships (National Council of Nonprofits, 2023).

Historical Context and Sector Trends

The history of fundraising in the U.S. nonprofit sector shows broad social and economic transformations. In the early 20th century, philanthropic models were dominated by elite foundations and federated campaigns such as the United Way. Over time, technological shifts, social movements, and donor expectations expanded the landscape of fundraising approaches (Zunz, 2012).

Fundraising has become more data-driven, decentralized, and democratized in the past two decades. The growth of online giving, peer-to-peer fundraising, and micro-donation platforms has created new opportunities for small nonprofits and everyday donors to take part in philanthropy. These digital tools not only have increased accessibility but also have helped organizations to reach wider, more diverse audiences. The COVID-19 pandemic pushed these trends even further, prompting many organizations to quickly adopt digital solutions and reimagine how they connect with their supporters (Giving USA Foundation, 2024).

Current trends demonstrate the importance of organizational adaptability:

12. Digital fundraising now accounts for nearly 13% of total charitable giving in the U.S. (Giving USA Foundation, 2024).

13. Donor retention remains a persistent challenge, with average annual retention hovering below 45% (Fundraising Effectiveness Project, 2023).

14. Equity in philanthropy is gaining attention, as donors and communities question how power, privilege, and access shape fundraising practices (Community-Centric Fundraising, 2023).

Nonprofit leaders today face more than just changes in technology and donor expectations—they must also grapple with deeper challenges posed by equity, inclusion, and the question of whose voices are represented in philanthropic spaces.

Ethics and Accountability in Fundraising

Fundraising practices must reflect the highest standards of transparency and integrity. Ethical lapses—such as misleading impact claims, donor manipulation, or mission drift to chase funding—can erode public trust and jeopardize organizational legitimacy (Edelman, 2023).

The Association of Fundraising Professionals (AFP) Code of Ethical Standards provides a comprehensive framework for responsible fundraising. Key principles include:

1. Honoring donor intent and confidentiality.

2. Accurately reporting financial need and program outcomes.

3. Avoiding undue influence or exploitation in solicitation practices (AFP, 2023).

Nonprofit leaders must also ensure that fundraising strategies are mission-aligned. Accepting funds from sources that contradict organizational values, or shifting programmatic focus solely to attract new dollars, will compromise long-term credibility. A mission-driven fundraising strategy begins with clarity of purpose and the courage to say no when opportunities threaten organizational integrity (Crutchfield & Grant, 2012).

Equity and Power in Development

Fundraising is not immune to the structural inequities present in society. Traditional fundraising models often concentrate power in the hands of major donors or institutional funders, marginalizing the voices of those served by the organization. A growing movement within the sector calls for a shift from extractive fundraising, focused on what can be taken from communities to community-centered fundraising, which emphasizes reciprocity, co-creation, and shared owner-ship (Community-Centric Fundraising, 2023).

Leaders committed to equity in fundraising must ask:

1. Who is making decisions about fundraising priorities and messaging?

2. Are we valuing relationships with grassroots donors as much as we value those with major funders?

3. How are we including the voices of beneficiaries in our development strategy?

By embedding equity in fundraising, nonprofit leaders can build more inclusive and sustainable financial systems that reflect the values of justice, dignity, and shared leadership (Villanueva, 2018).

Grant Writing Essentials

Grant writing is a foundational skill for nonprofit leaders who seek institutional funding to support programs, infrastructure, and in-novation. While often viewed as a technical task delegated to develop-ment staff, successful grant writing is, at its core, a leadership function. Success depends on aligning strategy with mission, communicating transparently, and remaining attuned to what funders value, all while being honest about the organization's actual capabilities.

Winning grants is about more than polished writing, it requires proving that an organization is prepared, accountable, and capable of making a difference. A strong proposal reflects and resonates with both the organization's mission and the funder's goals, showing a genuine alignment of purpose.

Types of Grant Funding

1. Understanding the major categories of grantmaking is essential to identifying appropriate opportunities:

2. Grants from foundations, whether private, family, or community-based, can take many forms, ranging from single-year awards to long-term funding commitments that span several years.

3. Corporate grants typically align with business interests or social responsibility goals, and may include both cash and in-kind or volunteer support.

4. Government grants, including federal, state, and local programs, are highly structured, and often require compliance with complex regulations.

5. Federated funds, such as those from the United Way or other pooled giving networks, may require collective impact alignment and community participation.

Each funding source carries its own expectations, reporting structures, and strategic implications. Leaders must evaluate the financial potential and the administrative and reputational costs of pursuing specific opportunities (Browning, 2020).

Anatomy of a Competitive Grant Proposal

While formats may vary, most grant applications include the following core components:

6. **Executive Summary:** Offers a clear, high-level snapshot of the funding request, summarizing the project's goals, proposed strategy, and expected impact.

7. **Need Statement:** Presents a persuasive argument for the proposed work, using relevant data, community input, and

contextual insight to define the issue or opportunity that the project aims to address.

8. **Organizational Background:** A narrative that builds trust by showcasing the nonprofit's track record, leadership, and alignment with the funder's values and priorities.

9. **Program Description:** Spells out the logistics of an organization's plans, detailing goals, activities, and projected outcomes. It often is grounded in a logic model or theory of change to illustrate the path to impact.

10. **Evaluation Plan:** Methodology for assessing outputs, outcomes, and impact, including tools, metrics, and responsible personnel.

11. **Budget and Justification:** A detailed financial plan demonstrating the application of funds and why they are necessary for success.

12. **Sustainability Plan:** Description of how the initiative will be sustained after the grant period ends.

The most effective proposals are simultaneously precise and persuasive. Such proposals avoid jargon, highlight measurable outcomes, and frame the organization as a capable and trustworthy steward of philanthropic investment (Karsh & Fox, 2019).

Strategic Fit and Funder Alignment

Successful grant-seeking begins with researching funders whose interests, values, and historical giving patterns align with the nonprofit's mission. Many grant applications are rejected not because of poor quality, but because of poor fit.

Leadership questions to consider before applying:

- Does this grant opportunity align with our strategic goals?
- Are we prepared to fulfill the administrative and reporting requirements?
- Would accepting this funding shift our mission or create a dependency?

Tools such as Foundation Directory Online, Instrumentl, and Grants.gov can support funder research, but must be paired with discernment. Funders increasingly prioritize alignment over volume, seeking deeper, more relational partnerships with fewer grantees (GEO, 2022).

Building Funder Relationships

Grant success rates improve dramatically when organizations build relationships with funders before applying. This may include:

- Attending funder-hosted webinars or community listening sessions.
- Reaching out with clarifying questions or expressions of interest.
- Inviting program officers for site visits or virtual updates.
- Demonstrating a willingness to learn from feedback and adapt accordingly.

What comes after the grant is awarded matters just as much as the initial overtures to the funder. Strong relationships with funders are built on regular communication, timely reporting, and a willingness to share both successes and setbacks. This level of transparency fosters trust and helps to create the foundation for long-term support. Some foundations invite grantees to co-create learning agendas, or to participate in cohort-based initiatives. Such opportunities extend influence and learning far beyond financial support (Center for Effective Philanthropy, 2023).

Common Pitfalls in Grant Writing

Even with the best of intentions, nonprofits can run into common, often avoidable, pitfalls during the grant writing process. These may include setting unrealistic or unproven goals, overlooking indirect costs that later strain the budget, or relying on vague language that doesn't clearly connect the project to the funder's priorities. Missed deadlines or incomplete applications, often the result of poor internal coordination, are also common issues. Implementing strong systems such as clear timelines, designated proposal leads, and internal peer reviews, can go a long way to prevent these challenges and to improve overall grant success.

Leadership Considerations

Executive leadership plays a vital role in ensuring that grant development is intentional, rooted in the mission, and positioned for long-term success. Such leadership includes:

- Participating in the cultivation of key funders.
- Supporting the development of strong program evaluation frameworks.
- Encouraging collaboration across departments for integrated proposals.
- Modeling ethical standards for how funds are pursued, represented, and utilized.

At its heart, grant writing is about much more than simply securing funding, it's an opportunity to advance the mission, build credibility, and foster meaningful partnerships by pursuing well-researched, strategically aligned funding opportunities.

Engaging Donors and Building Relationships

Engaging individual donors is more than a tactic, it's at the heart of what makes nonprofit work sustainable over time. While large grants and institutional gifts can provide a necessary boost, it's the steady support of individuals who believe in the mission that often carries the work forward. These relationships are built on more than money, they're rooted in trust, shared values, and ongoing communication.

Donors, no matter how much they give, often become some of the most dedicated champions of the cause. They spread the word, vouch for the organization's credibility, and strengthen its presence in the community. Such support doesn't happen by accident, it evolves from an organization's commitment of time, intention, and a genuine effort to stay connected, listen well, and follow through.

Understanding Donor Motivation

Donors give for many reasons, including personal experience, belief in a cause, desire for social recognition, or alignment with values. The decision to give is often emotional before it is rational. According to research by the Lilly Family School of Philanthropy (2022), donors' top motivations include:

- A sense of moral obligation to help others.
- The belief that their gift will make a difference.
- Trust in the organization's leadership and effectiveness.

Meaningful donor engagement starts with recognizing what drives supporters to give, then shaping communication to reflect those motivations. Defining donors by their giving history, communication preferences, and interests enables personalized outreach that respects the donor's intent and identity (Tempel, Seiler, & Burlingame, 2016).

The Donor Journey: From Awareness to Loyalty

Effective donor engagement requires guiding them through a meaningful journey, one that begins with discovery and, over time, builds toward a deep, enduring commitment to your mission. This journey often unfolds in a few key stages:

- **Acquisition** – The first step is helping new supporters find your organization. This could occur through a community event, an online campaign, a personal referral, or even a social media post that sparks curiosity.
- **Cultivation** – Once a connection is established, the relationship needs care. Thoughtful storytelling, honest communication, and regular updates deepen the potential donor's interest and trust.
- **Solicitation** – When the time is right, making the ask matters. A clear, timely request that ties directly to your mission invites donors to take meaningful action.
- **Stewardship** – The real work of gratitude and accountability comes after the gift has been made. Showing donors how their contributions make a difference not only builds trust, but also inspires future support.

Each stage offers an opportunity for meaningful connection. For example, a personalized thank-you video or handwritten note after a first gift can significantly increase the likelihood of a second donation (Penelope Burk Research, 2021).

Building Authentic Relationships

Trust is the currency of effective fundraising. Donors are more likely to give, and to continue giving, when they feel known, valued, and respected. This requires:

- Transparent communication about how funds are used.

- Timely reporting of outcomes and challenges.
- Invitations to engage beyond financial support (e.g., volunteering, advising, hosting).

Authenticity matters. Overly transactional or generic communication can damage relationships. Conversely, when nonprofits treat donors as partners rather than ATMs, they deepen loyalty and increase lifetime value (Burnett, 2021).

Leadership's Role in Donor Engagement

While development staff often manage day-to-day donor relations, leadership sets the tone and culture. Executive directors and board members play critical roles in:

- Hosting cultivation events or site visits.
- Participating in major gift solicitations.
- Expressing gratitude in internal and external communications.
- Building a culture in which fundraising is viewed as mission-aligned, not ancillary.

Leaders should also advocate for investment in donor relationship infrastructure—such as CRM systems, communications platforms, and staff training—that supports personalization and long-term stewardship (AFP, 2023).

Strategic Communication Tools

Effective communication with donors is strategic, consistent, and multi-channel. Common tools include:

- **Newsletters (print or email):** Ideal for updates and storytelling.

- **Impact reports:** Formal documents highlighting outcomes, lessons learned, and gratitude.
- **Social media:** Informal, real-time engagement that reinforces brand identity.
- **One-on-one calls or meetings:** Personalized interactions that foster a deeper connection.

Tailoring messages to different donor groups makes outreach more meaningful. A first-time donor might get a welcome email series, while a major donor could receive personalized reports or direct updates from leadership.

The Role of Storytelling

Data informs, but stories inspire. Sharing authentic narratives about program beneficiaries, volunteers, or community impact makes the case for giving more compelling. Research shows donors are more responsive to emotionally resonant stories than to statistics alone (Breeze, 2017).

Effective stories:

- Focus on people, not programs.
- Show transformation, not just need.
- Reflect shared values and desired outcomes.

Pairing stories with outcome data (e.g., "because of your support, 85% of clients secured stable housing") offers a powerful combination of heart and evidence.

Equity Considerations in Donor Engagement

Traditional fundraising models often give preference to wealth and reinforce inequitable power dynamics. Community-Centric

Fundraising (2023) calls for approaches that:

- Recognize and value small-dollar donors.
- Avoid transactional language that objectifies recipients or glorifies donors.
- Center community voice in messaging and strategy.

Leaders committed to equity should regularly examine who is being prioritized, who is being excluded, and how engagement strategies align with organizational values of justice and inclusion.

Community-Based Fundraising Initiatives

Community-based fundraising draws power from the connections, energy, and resources that already exist within a local area. It's built on the idea that everyone has something to contribute, whether in time, money, or networks, and that real impact occurs when people feel included and invested. These efforts foster a sense of shared ownership, in which supporting the mission becomes a collective effort rather than the job of a few. Unlike major donor or institutional fundraising, community-based efforts emphasize breadth over depth, building many modest contributions into robust funding, awareness, and advocacy vehicles.

For nonprofit leaders, community-based fundraising is about more than raising funds, it's an opportunity to strengthen local ties, promote equity, and demonstrate that the organization is listening and responding to the community's needs. When done thoughtfully, it reinforces a powerful message: philanthropy isn't limited to those with deep pockets. It's a shared responsibility and a meaningful way for everyone to contribute to lasting change.

Characteristics and Benefits

Community-based fundraising has several distinguishing features:

13. **Inclusive Participation:** Anyone can contribute, regardless of income level.

14. **Local Relevance:** Campaigns reflect community identity, culture, and needs.

15. **Grassroots Ownership:** Donors often become advocates and ambassadors.

16. **Narrative Power:** Community stories amplify urgency and impact.

17. **Social Capital:** Campaigns can strengthen networks and civic cohesion.

Beyond financial outcomes, community-based fundraising increases visibility, strengthens trust, and positions the nonprofit as a community-anchored institution (Gittell & Vidal, 1998).

Common Community Fundraising Models

While community fundraising can take many forms, certain approaches tend to resonate more deeply and bring people together in meaningful ways.

1. **Special events** such as fun runs, benefit concerts, auctions, or neighborhood festivals create shared experiences that attract and engage a wide range of supporters. They're a great way to raise both money and visibility. That said, they require a great deal of planning and hands-on effort, so it's important to weigh the potential return against the resources that they demand.

2. **Giving Circles:** Groups of individuals pool their resources

and make collective decisions about where to give. These democratized models of philanthropy encourage peer learning and shared decision-making (Bearman, Carboni, & Eikenberry, 2013).

3. **Honor Campaigns:** Fundraising in honor or memory of someone can activate personal networks and link giving to shared experiences or milestones.

4. **Peer-to-Peer (P2P) Campaigns:** Supporters create fundraising pages to engage friends, family, and colleagues. These decentralized efforts often reach new audiences and, using the right tools and training, can be highly scalable.

5. **Community Matching Funds:** Local businesses or donors match community contributions during a specified period, incentivizing participation and amplifying impact.

6. **Pop-Up and Place-Based Appeals:** Tabling at local markets, hosting neighborhood dinners, or organizing house parties are hyperlocal approaches that meet people where they are.

Engaging Volunteers as Fundraising Ambassadors

One of the greatest strengths of community-based fundraising is the degree to which it depends on people—not just to donate, but to lead. When volunteers are trusted and equipped to step into fundraising roles, they often become some of the most powerful ambassadors for the mission. Their personal connections and passion can extend the organization's reach and build trust in ways that formal campaigns alone can't always achieve. This approach includes:

1. Training supporters in how to share the organization's story.

2. Providing toolkits for outreach and solicitation.

3. Recognizing contributions beyond financial gifts (e.g., time, talent, social reach).

Research shows that campaigns with strong peer leadership outperform those managed solely by staff, particularly when volunteers reflect the diversity of the broader community (Nonprofit Quarterly, 2020).

Technology and Community Engagement

Digital platforms have expanded the reach of community-based fundraising, allowing small, place-based campaigns to connect with broader audiences. Tools like Classy, GoFundMe Charity, and Givebutter support mobile giving, social sharing, and real-time donation tracking. Text-to-give and QR code systems are handy at live events.

However, technology should amplify, not replace, community relationships. Leaders must ensure that digital tools are culturally and linguistically accessible, mobile-optimized, and aligned with the organization's tone and values (NTEN, 2023).

Leadership's Role in Community Fundraising

Executive and board leadership can play a vital role by:

1. Publicly and visibly endorsing grassroots campaigns.

2. Attending community-led events.

3. Highlighting the value of small-dollar donors.

4. Allocating staff time and infrastructure support for volunteer-led initiatives.

Leadership must also guard against tokenism. Community participation should be genuine, not symbolic. If fundraising activities solicit community contributions without including those same voices in planning and decision-making, they risk being perceived as exploitive or performative (Guo & Saxton, 2010).

Equity and Accessibility

To truly reflect the spirit of community, fundraising efforts need to be inclusive from the start. Issues such as language barriers, transportation challenges, limited internet access, or even the cost of attending an event can prevent some people from participation. Being intentional about equity requires identifying those barriers and finding ways to lower them, for example:

1. Offering donation options that don't require extra fees, choosing venues that are accessible, and scheduling events at convenient times that work for families. Small choices like these can make a big difference in who feels welcome and able to participate.

2. Translating materials and providing interpretation at events.

3. Providing non-monetary participation options (e.g., volunteering, skill-sharing).

When performed in an equitable manner, community-based fundraising fosters a culture of shared ownership and accountability, positioning the organization as a partner rather than as a service provider.

Digital Fundraising: Crowdfunding, Peer-to-Peer Campaigns, and Social Media Strategies

Digital fundraising has reshaped the way nonprofits connect with their supporters. It's made giving easier, has extended the reach of campaigns, and has allowed organizations to communicate in real time with their communities. As traditional models shift, digital tools offer nonprofit leaders new ways to tell their stories, build relationships, and expand their impact across regions and communities.

Leaders must understand the capabilities and limitations of digital tools while ensuring that online engagement aligns with the organizational mission and values.

The Digital Landscape

Digital giving now accounts for a significant and growing share of charitable contributions. In 2023, online donations in the U.S. increased by 10.5%, with mobile giving comprising nearly 30% of all digital transactions (M+R Benchmarks, 2023). Social media platforms, email campaigns, and donation portals have become essential infrastructure for most fundraising programs.

Core benefits of digital fundraising include:

1. **Scalability:** Campaigns can quickly reach thousands of potential donors.

2. **Cost-efficiency:** Digital appeals are generally less expensive than direct mail or events.

3. **Real-time analytics:** Immediate feedback enables agile campaign adjustments.

4. **Donor convenience:** Supporters can give quickly via smartphones, tablets, or social media.

Despite its many strengths, digital fundraising must be designed with equity in mind. Access to the internet, familiarity with platforms, and comfort with online transactions vary across demographic groups

(NTEN, 2023).

Crowdfunding

Crowdfunding campaigns involve raising small amounts of money from many people, typically through time-limited online campaigns hosted on platforms such as GoFundMe Charity, Global Giving, or Classy. These campaigns often focus on specific projects or urgent needs and rely heavily on social sharing to gain traction.

Effective crowdfunding campaigns share several characteristics:

1. A compelling, emotionally resonant story.

2. A clear and specific goal (e.g., "Help us raise $15,000 for a youth summer program").

3. Strong visuals (photos, short videos, infographics).

4. Frequent updates and gratitude messaging.

A Charitable Giving Research Center study found that crowdfunding campaigns with video content raised 105% more than those without video content (CGRC, 2022). This reflects the power of narrative and visual communication in digital spaces.

Peer-to-Peer (P2P) Campaigns

Peer-to-peer fundraising puts the power in the hands of your supporters. By creating their own fundraising pages, using any one of a variety of P2P platforms, and by reaching out to friends, family, and colleagues, they help to spread the word and raise money for their causes. It's a powerful approach to grow both visibility and trust, because when donors become fundraisers, they bring their passion and personal stories with them.

P2P strategies include:

1. **Birthday or milestone giving:** Encouraging supporters to solicit donations in lieu of gifts.

2. **Athletic challenges:** Participants collect pledges for races, hikes, or fitness goals.

3. **Themed challenges:** Viral campaigns such as the "Ice Bucket Challenge" (ALS Association) demonstrate how creativity and social sharing can drive massive results.

Successful peer-to-peer campaigns require infrastructure:

1. A user-friendly, mobile-optimized platform.

2. Clear messaging and branding.

3. Fundraiser toolkits (sample emails, social media templates).

4. Recognition and support for fundraisers throughout the campaign.

According to Blackbaud (2023), organizations that offer training and support for peer fundraisers realize 27% higher average donations per campaign.

Social Media Strategies

Social media platforms—Facebook, Instagram, TikTok, LinkedIn, and others—are now critical channels for digital fundraising and donor engagement. These platforms are not merely for promotion, but provide spaces for storytelling, community building, and direct action.

Best practices in social media fundraising include:

1. **Consistent branding and voice:** Posts should reflect orga-

nizational identity and values.

2. **Platform-native content:** Videos on TikTok, reels on Instagram, and stories on Facebook perform better than cross-posted content.

3. **Call-to-action clarity:** Every post should offer a next step—donate, share, comment, or attend.

4. **Timing and frequency:** Strategic posting schedules aligned with audience behavior increase engagement.

Social media campaigns are most effective when integrated with broader digital strategies, including email marketing, website content, and donor segmentation. Each platforms' analytics tools can inform strategies designed to increase reach and conversion.

Risks and Considerations

Digital fundraising also presents challenges:

1. **Donor data ownership:** Some platforms restrict access to donor information, limiting stewardship.

2. **Platform fees:** Processing and platform charges, if not absorbed, can reduce net revenue.

3. **Short attention spans:** Digital audiences move quickly, requiring short, visually engaging appeals.

Leaders must also ensure that digital campaigns adhere to ethical fundraising standards, including transparency about how funds will be used and respect for donor privacy.

Equity in Digital Access

Not all communities engage equally with digital platforms. Relying solely on digital fundraising can exclude supporters who lack consistent internet access, digital literacy, or language support. To mitigate this:

1. Offer multilingual donation pages and materials.

2. Use SMS/text-to-give options for mobile-only audiences.

3. Pair digital campaigns with in-person or hybrid outreach.

4. Equity-focused digital design ensures that online fundraising is genuinely inclusive, expanding access to philanthropy rather than reinforcing digital divides (NTEN, 2023).

Corporate Partnerships: Structuring Win-Win Sponsorships and CSR Collaborations

Corporate partnerships can be a powerful element of a diversified fundraising strategy, offering nonprofits access to new resources, expanded networks, and long-term support. As businesses increasingly prioritize corporate social responsibility (CSR), they seek value-aligned nonprofit collaborators to help them to achieve their social impact goal while strengthening community ties and brand identity.

For nonprofit leaders, the key to successful corporate partnerships is structuring strategic, equitable, and mission-consistent relationships. These collaborations must serve mutual interests while protecting the organization's integrity, reputation, and autonomy.

The Rise of Corporate Social Responsibility

Corporate social responsibility (CSR) has come a long way, evolving from a bid for good publicity to an integral aspect of the ways in which companies conduct business. Today, many companies are expected to make a positive impact in their communities while still meeting their financial goals. In a 2022 Deloitte study, 77% of consumers reported they are more likely to support companies that align with their social values (Deloitte, 2022). This trend has driven a surge in philanthropic giving, employee volunteering, and cause marketing initiatives by companies of all sizes.

Corporate support for nonprofits typically takes several forms:

1. Cash sponsorships for events, campaigns, or programs.

2. In-kind donations, such as equipment, software, or professional services.

3. Employee giving and volunteerism programs.

4. Matching gift programs to amplify employee contributions.

5. Cause-related marketing and co-branded campaigns.

6. Long-term strategic partnerships tied to shared outcomes or metrics.

Leaders must assess each model's implications and determine how best to integrate corporate support into broader fundraising and impact strategies.

Aligning Mission and Brand

Not all corporate support is beneficial. Partnerships must align with the nonprofit's mission, values, and public image. A misaligned partnership may yield short-term financial gain at the cost of long-term credibility or stakeholder trust.

Leaders should evaluate potential partners through questions such as:

1. Does the company's core business or industry align with our values?

2. Has it demonstrated a genuine commitment to social responsibility?

3. How might its reputation affect our brand among donors, clients, or funders?

4. Will the partnership promote or compromise our mission integrity?

The 2023 Edelman Trust Barometer found that 61% of consumers distrust "purpose-washing," where companies overstate or misrepresent their philanthropic efforts (Edelman, 2023). Nonprofits that endorse these companies risk reputational harm unless the collaboration is authentic, transparent, and accountable.

Structuring Sponsorships and Agreements

Strong partnerships don't happen by chance, they're built on clear communication, shared goals, and a sense of mutual benefit. Putting those expectations in writing, using tools such as Memoranda of Understanding (MOUs) or sponsorship agreements, helps keep everyone on the same page and makes it easier to remain accountable as the work moves forward.

Key components of partnership agreements include:

1. Roles and responsibilities of each party.

2. Funding amounts and disbursement schedules.

3. Use of logos and brand assets.

4. Reporting and impact measurement requirements.

5. Duration and renewal terms.

6. Termination clauses for conflict or misalignment.

Nonprofits also should define what they offer in return for corporate support such as logo placement, social media promotion, recognition at events, or inclusion in press materials. These benefits must be proportional to the sponsorship level and appropriate to the organization's audience and values.

The Role of Relationship Management

Corporate partnerships are most beneficial when they are viewed as ongoing relationships rather than one-time deals. Remaining in contact through regular updates, sharing impact stories, and inviting partners to be part of events or initiatives helps to sustain a strong connection. This kind of thoughtful engagement builds trust over time, often leading to deeper, longer-lasting support.

Nonprofit leadership, especially executive directors and board members, plays a crucial role in:

1. Initiating and cultivating corporate relationships.
2. Representing the organization at corporate events or meetings.
3. Framing the partnership as a strategic alliance, not just a funding request.

According to the Council on Foundations (2023), partnerships with strong executive involvement are 35% more likely to yield multi-year support.

Employee Engagement Programs

Many corporations support employee giving, matching gift programs, and employer-sponsored volunteerism. These programs can significantly increase revenue and visibility when nonprofits are listed in employer portals or partner directories.

Strategies to optimize employee engagement include:

1. Ensuring the organization is registered with major giving platforms (e.g., Benevity, Your Cause).

2. Promoting matching gift opportunities in donor communications.

3. Offering meaningful, skill-based volunteer opportunities for employee groups.

These efforts require coordination with HR departments, community relations/marketing teams, and systems to track participation and recognition.

Risk Management and Ethical Considerations

Corporate support is not without risk. Potential pitfalls include:

1. Perceived appropriation or influence over programming.

2. Conflicts of interest in decision-making or governance.

3. Community backlash for partnering with controversial industries (e.g., fossil fuels, tobacco).

To mitigate these risks, nonprofit boards should establish gift acceptance and partnership screening policies that:

1. Define prohibited sources or industries.

2. Outline due diligence procedures.

3. Require staff and board review for high-value or high-profile partnerships.

A transparent process for evaluating corporate partners protects the organization and reinforces its commitment to ethical leadership (Independent Sector, 2023).

Donor Retention: Building Loyalty Through Stewardship and Impact Reporting

Donor retention is one of the most critical, yet underprioritized, aspects of nonprofit fundraising. While acquiring new donors garners significant attention and resources, sustaining relationships with existing supporters yields far greater long-term value. Research consistently shows that retaining even 10% more donors can increase lifetime giving by up to 200% (Sargeant & Shang, 2016).

Effective donor retention is rooted in stewardship, the intentional cultivating of ongoing relationships that communicate appreciation, demonstrate impact, and foster mutual trust. For nonprofit leaders, stewardship is not a transactional follow-up, but a strategic leadership function that reflects the organization's values and accountability.

The Donor Retention Challenge

Even though keeping donors engaged is critical, many nonprofits struggle with it. According to the Fundraising Effectiveness Project (2023), the average donor retention rate in the U.S. has been stuck around 43% and is even lower—under 20%—for first-time donors. These numbers illustrate how challenging it can be to transform an initial gift into an ongoing relationship. Many organizations are discovering that, although attracting new donors is important, sustaining a connection with them over time takes just as much attention and care.

Contributors to low retention include:

1. Lack of personalized communication.

2. Infrequent or inconsistent outreach.

3. Unclear or unconvincing demonstrations of impact.

4. Perceived donor fatigue or solicitation overload.

These challenges can be addressed, but they demand leadership attention, adequate systems, and a culture that values relationships over revenue.

Principles of Donor Stewardship

At its heart, stewardship is about respecting the trust that donors have placed in your organization, and showing them, through your actions, that their support truly matters.

Effective stewardship involves four key principles:

1. **Acknowledgment** – Timely, sincere recognition of each gift, regardless of size.

2. **Transparency** – Clear communication about how donations are used, including successes and challenges.

3. **Gratitude** – Authentic expressions of thanks, delivered through multiple channels and organizational voices.

4. **Reciprocity** – Providing opportunities for donors to learn, ask questions, and be part of the impact journey, not only as financial contributors but also mission partners.

These principles apply not only to major donors, but also to monthly givers, small-dollar contributors, and peer-to-peer fundraisers. Stewardship must be inclusive, not elitist (Burnett, 2021).

Tactical Tools for Donor Retention

Several tools and practices have been proven effective in retaining donors:

1. **Thank-You Letters:** Handwritten or customized digital notes issued within 48 hours of a gift dramatically improve retention.

2. **Impact Reports:** Annual or semi-annual publications highlighting results, stories, and future plans.

3. **Donor Spotlights:** Featuring supporters in newsletters or social media as a form of public recognition.

4. **Personal Calls:** Board members or staff calling to thank donors strengthens personal connections.

5. **Special Updates:** Behind-the-scenes briefings, sneak peeks, or progress notes to make donors feel like insiders.

Multi-channel strategies employing email, phone, mail, and social media ensure that diverse audiences are reached in their preferred formats. Segmentation based on giving history or interests allows for tailored messaging and prioritization of high-risk or high-value donors (AFP, 2023).

Measuring Retention and Engagement

Nonprofits must track and analyze donor retention metrics with the same rigor as that which they apply to acquisition or revenue goals. Key indicators include:

1. First-time vs. repeat donor retention rates

2. Monthly donor retention

3. Lapsed donor reactivation

4.   Average donor lifespan

5.   Lifetime donor value

These metrics can be tracked using donor management systems (e.g., Salesforce, Bloomerang, Little Green Light), many of which offer built-in retention dashboards and engagement scoring tools.

Leadership should regularly review this data at the board or executive level and use it to inform fundraising strategy, staffing, and goal setting (Blackbaud Institute, 2022).

The Power of Impact Reporting

Donors give because they want to make a difference. Demonstrating how their gifts have translated into outcomes is among the most effective retention strategies. Strong impact reporting includes:

1.   Quantitative results (e.g., meals served, clients housed, graduation rates).

2.   Qualitative stories (e.g., client testimonials, staff reflections).

3.   Visual content (e.g., infographics, photos, videos).

4.   Contextual framing (e.g., alignment with broader community change.)

Good donor reports should speak plainly, celebrate progress, and be honest about what remains to be done. Most importantly, the reports should show the ways in which donor support is making a real difference. Being transparent, even about challenges or what didn't go as planned, helps to build trust and demonstrates the organization's commitment to learning and growing (GEO, 2022).

Leadership's Role in Cultivating Loyalty

Executive directors and senior leaders play a critical role in donor retention by:

1. Publicly acknowledging donors in speeches, reports, or videos.

2. Expressing gratitude in internal and external communications.

3. Investing in systems, staff, and training that support stewardship.

4. Holding the organization accountable to high standards of transparency.

Boards also can support retention by participating in thank-you calls, writing notes, or reviewing retention data quarterly.

In a sector where public trust is fragile and donor expectations are rising; stewardship is not optional—it is a leadership imperative.

Micro-Philanthropy: Engaging Small-Dollar Donors at Scale

Micro-philanthropy refers to mobilizing large numbers of individuals to contribute small amounts—often $1 to $100—to support a shared mission. While each contribution may be modest, the aggregate impact can be transformative. Beyond revenue, micro-philanthropy builds broad-based community ownership, democratizes philanthropy, and strengthens public trust in the nonprofit sector.

In today's uncertain economy and evolving philanthropic landscape, small-dollar donors offer a big opportunity. While they may not give large amounts individually, together they represent a powerful force. In fact, nearly 60% of U.S. donors give less than $250 a year, according to the Lilly Family School of Philanthropy (2023). This is a reminder that engaging everyday donors, often overlooked, can be key to long-term sustainability and broader community support.

The Case for Micro-Philanthropy

Leaders sometimes underestimate the value of small-dollar donors, prioritizing major gifts and institutional support. However, organizations that build a culture of inclusivity and scale among micro-givers benefit from:

1. Revenue stability through high-volume, diversified contributions.

2. Increased visibility via social sharing and peer advocacy.

3. Lower donor acquisition costs through automated and digital platforms.

4. Mission alignment with equitable access to philanthropy.

Perhaps most importantly, micro-philanthropy invites participation from people who may not have large financial means but who possess deep commitment, lived experience, or community connection (Villanueva, 2018).

Effective Micro-Giving Models

Several models have proven effective in cultivating small-dollar giving at scale:

1. **Monthly Giving Programs:** Sustainers provide reliable, recurring revenue. Even $10/month donors, when retained, yield high lifetime value. Programs should be easy to join,

upgrade, or pause, with recognition that matches the donor's loyalty, not just their gift size (Burnett, 2021).

2. **Round-Up Campaigns:** Donors round up purchases to the nearest dollar to support a cause. These campaigns are particularly effective when embedded in e-commerce or retail partnerships.

3. **Micro-Donations via Mobile:** Text-to-give, QR codes, and mobile-optimized donation pages reduce friction in giving. According to Nonprofit Tech for Good (2023), 65% of small-dollar online gifts are now made via mobile devices.

4. **"Give What You Can" Appeals:** Messaging that removes minimum thresholds ("$3 makes a difference") invites broader participation and reflects values of equity and accessibility.

5. **Social media Micro-Campaigns:** Viral hashtags, Instagram donation stickers, and Facebook birthday fundraisers allow users to give and invite others to join. These campaigns excel at recruiting new donors and expanding reach.

Messaging and Engagement Strategies

Micro-giving campaigns succeed when they emphasize:

- **Collective impact:** "Together, 500 people gave $5 to fund the summer program."
- **Donor dignity:** Affirming that small gifts matter—and matter deeply.
- **Urgency and relevance:** Tying appeals to immediate needs or time-bound goals.
- **Low friction:** One-click giving, Apple Pay, and donation forms with pre-filled amounts.

Tone and language matter. Avoid "entry-level donor" language that implies hierarchy or insufficiency. Instead, use inclusive framing such as "community investor" or "impact partner."

Recognition and Stewardship

Small-dollar donors deserve meaningful appreciation, even if not high-touch. Stewardship strategies include:

1. Digital thank-you messages with real-time impact visuals.

2. Collective recognition (e.g., "Wall of 1,000 Founders").

3. Tiered incentives (e.g. early access to reports, digital badges, or swag).

4. Invitation to co-create or vote on small projects (participatory giving).

Organizations that treat small-dollar donors with the same care and clarity given to donors often see higher retention, increased advocacy, and eventual gift upgrades (Sargeant & Shang, 2016).

Technology and Infrastructure

Scaling micro-philanthropy requires streamlined systems. Recommended tools and features include:

1. CRM segmentation for small-dollar recurring and one-time givers.

2. Automated workflows for acknowledgment, reminders, and re-engagement.

3. Mobile-first platforms to support giving via smartphone.

4. Data analytics dashboards to track conversion rates, donor churn, and lifetime value.

Platforms such as Classy, Givebutter, and Donorbox offer specialized features for micro-giving campaigns, including gamification, real-time tracking, and social integration.

Equity and Access in Small-Dollar Giving

When building a micro-philanthropy strategy, leaders need to think about equity from the start. The goal is to make giving accessible to everyone, but factors such as limited internet access, language barriers, or not having a credit card can pose obstacles. Addressing these challenges helps ensure that all supporters have a fair chance to participate. To improve equity:

1. Offer offline giving options (e.g., cash jars, pledge cards).
2. Translate giving materials into community languages.
3. Clarify that all gift sizes are equally valued.

Avoid practices that over-extract from marginalized groups without offering voice or participation.

When rooted in values of justice and shared ownership, micro-philanthropy becomes a powerful vehicle, not only for generating revenue, but also for solidarity and transformation.

Equity and Power in Fundraising

Fundraising is not neutral, it is shaped by longstanding systems of power, privilege, and access. While philanthropy aspires to promote justice and public good, it often replicates the very inequities that it seeks to address. For nonprofit leaders, embracing equity in fundraising requires more than inclusion in donor lists or translation of appeal letters; it demands a fundamental reexamination of the ways in which resources are raised and allocated, and who gets to decide.

This section explores how traditional fundraising practices can perpetuate disparities and offers alternative models rooted in transparency, shared leadership, and community accountability.

The Power Dynamics of Philanthropy

Traditionally, fundraising has placed a large amount of power in the hands of major donors, foundations, and large institutions, many of whom are far removed from the communities that their funding is meant to support. This imbalance can lead to real challenges, such as:

1. Misaligned priorities, which cause programs to be shaped more by funder interests than by community needs.

2. Restricted funding, which can limit an organization's ability to adapt or try new ideas.

3. Lack of representation, in which the voices of those most affected are left out of key decisions.

4. Extractive storytelling, through which clients' experiences are exploited to generate donations without consent or reciprocity.

According to the Race to Lead Initiative (2022), 60% of nonprofit leaders of color report feeling pressure to alter programming to meet funder expectations, even when it conflicts with community needs. These pressures reflect more profound structural inequities with regard to control of philanthropic capital.

Equity-Aligned Fundraising Practices

Increasingly, nonprofit leaders are rethinking how fundraising is done, shifting away from models that prioritize donor preferences above other concerns, and moving toward approaches rooted in transparency, inclusion, and shared power.

One key shift is emphasizing transparency and informed consent in storytelling. This requires asking, not assuming, and ensuring that those whose stories are shared understand how their personal histories will be used and that they feel respected in the process.

Another shift is the redistribution of decision-making power, giving frontline staff, community members, and program participants a real voice in shaping fundraising efforts. Whether this is accomplished through advisory committees or collaborative planning, these individuals' insight helps to ground campaigns in real experiences.

Community-Centric Fundraising (2023) encourages this shift, moving away from the mindset of transactional giving and hierarchical donor relationships. Instead, CCF views donors as partners in collective liberation, a collaborative process through which fundraising becomes a shared effort, not just a financial exchange.

To implement these ideas, nonprofit leaders can:

1. Practice shared governance by inviting people with lived experience into fundraising conversations. Their participation can occur through advisory groups, storytelling teams, or even board service and their perspectives help ensure that messages reflect real community needs.

2. Design inclusive campaigns by co-creating appeals with the communities being served. When language, visuals, and outreach strategies reflect people's identities and values, campaigns feel more authentic and become more effective.

This form of fundraising doesn't only raise money. It builds trust, strengthens community bonds, and brings the work closer to the people whom it is meant to serve.

Equity-Aligned Fundraising Practices

Nonprofit leaders can adopt a range of practices to advance equity in development work:

1. **Shared Governance:** Include community members and program participants on fundraising advisory committees or boards. Their insights can improve messaging and ensure alignment with lived realities.

2. **Inclusive Campaign Design:** Co-create campaigns with those served by the organization, ensuring that language, imagery, and appeals all reflect community identity and values.

3. **Ethical Storytelling:** Use consent-based practices for testimonials. Empower clients and staff to actively share their own narratives rather than being depicted as passive recipients.

4. **Transparent Reporting:** Clearly report where money goes, who makes funding decisions, and how community voices are integrated in planning.

Redistribution Commitments: Allocate a portion of unrestricted funding to grassroots partners, mutual aid networks, or emergent community needs.

These practices foster equity, build authenticity, deepen trust, and position the organization as a credible agent of systemic change

(GEO, 2022).

Navigating Donor Pushback

Some donors may feel unsure or even push back when faced with equity-focused fundraising approaches, particularly if they are accustomed to more traditional models in which their gifts earned the donors recognition or decision-making influence. Leaders should anticipate such reactions and prepare to respond by:

1.   Framing changes as being aligned with mission and values.

2.   Providing educational opportunities (e.g., donor roundtables, webinars on equity).

3.   Offering alternative engagement paths (e.g., listening sessions, participatory grantmaking).

It's important to make clear the fact that embracing equity doesn't involve excluding people from the process. Instead, it widens the circle. It makes room for more voices, centers community perspectives, and ensures that power is shared in ways that are fair and inclusive.

Leadership Imperatives

Building a more equitable approach to fundraising begins with leadership. Executive teams and board members set the tone, not only through their words, but through the priorities that they champion and the choices that they make every day. This process includes:

1.   Ensuring the leadership team reflects the diversity of the communities served by the organization.

2.   Investing in ongoing equity training and building staff capacity to lead inclusive efforts.

3.   Setting clear goals for donor engagement that prioritize inclusion and relationship-building over hierarchy or exclusivity.

4.   Transforming equity from a value into an integral part of the organization's everyday practice.

5.   Evaluating fundraising metrics through an equity lens and asking relevant questions about the process (e.g., who gives, who benefits, who is centered?).

According to the National Committee for Responsive Philanthropy (2023), organizations that implement equity-centered fundraising strategies report higher community satisfaction, stronger donor retention among Gen Z and Millennials, and greater resilience during crises.

Building a Culture of Philanthropy

A culture of philanthropy is one in which fundraising is understood, not as the responsibility of a single department, but as a shared organizational value and practice. In such cultures, everyone—from board members and executive leadership to program staff and volunteers—embraces the role of ambassador, advocate, and steward of the mission.

This approach stands in stark contrast to organizations in which fundraising is treated as an afterthought and is kept separate from the rest of the work or is not fully understood. In organizations with a strong culture of philanthropy, fundraising is perceived to be a shared responsibility. This culture unites people together around a central mission, builds trust with donors, and helps to ensure that the organization can continue to make an impact for the long haul.

Defining a Culture of Philanthropy

According to the Evelyn and Walter Haas, Jr. Fund (2016), a culture of philanthropy is characterized by four core elements:

1. Shared responsibility for development across the organization.

2. Integration of fundraising into the overall mission and strategy.

3. A deep belief in relationship-building, not just transactions.

4. Organizational systems and structures that support donor engagement.

In this model, fundraising is viewed as a form of service, not as persuasion or pressure, and donors are viewed as partners in social change.

Shifting Organizational Mindsets

Developing a culture of philanthropy requires deliberate leadership. It begins with reframing internal narratives:

1. From "development's job" to "everyone's job"

2. From "asking for money" to "inviting people to invest in impact"

3. From "soliciting" to "cultivating mission alignment"

Leaders must model this mindset shift by speaking openly and positively about fundraising, celebrating donor engagement across all staff levels, and ensuring that fundraising goals are embedded in strategic planning, rather than being treated as an afterthought (Tempel, Seiler, & Burlingame, 2016).

Board Engagement and Ownership

Boards play a vital role in shaping how an organization approaches fundraising, yet many board members feel unsure about organizational expectations or are hesitant to become involved. That's why it is crucial that organizations offer the right support and guidance to their board members.

This can include:

1. Offering training and one-on-one coaching to build confidence and skills.

2. Setting clear, realistic expectations for giving and involvement.

3. Recognizing and celebrating both the time and money contributed by board members.

4. Involving board members in stewardship efforts, not just asking for donations.

When board members feel equipped and supported, they're more likely to embrace their role in fundraising. According to BoardSource's Leading with Intent report (2021), organizations with a strong culture of philanthropy at the board level are not only more likely to meet fundraising goals, but they're also better at building lasting relationships with high-impact donors.

Staff Engagement and Cross-Department Collaboration

Creating a culture of philanthropy also involves empowering non-development staff to contribute meaningfully to donor engagement. This includes:

5. Training program staff to talk about their work with funders.

1. Encouraging staff to share client stories and impact data.

2. Recognizing internal teams for their role in stewardship (e.g., timely data, welcoming site visits).

When staff understand that their work directly influences donor satisfaction and retention, they become more invested in organizational sustainability (Burnett, 2021).

Internal Systems and Structures

Infrastructure supports culture. A true culture of philanthropy requires:

1. CRMs that allow for organization-wide notes and engagement tracking.

2. Regular cross-team meetings that include development updates.

3. Shared performance metrics that reflect both programmatic and fundraising success.

4. Communication calendars that integrate donor engagement with program activities.

Donor stewardship should not exist in a vacuum. Organizations that integrate it into operations—from impact measurement to storytelling—build more resilient and adaptive systems (Blackbaud Institute, 2022).

Celebrating Giving and Gratitude

Celebration reinforces culture. Organizations that visibly express appreciation for donors, board members, staff, and community supporters create environments of abundance and inclusion. Practices may include:

1. Annual gratitude events or open houses

2. Public donor acknowledgments (with consent)

3. Stories that link donor contributions to tangible outcomes

4. Rituals of appreciation within team meetings or newsletters

Cultures rooted in gratitude foster loyalty, reduce burnout, and reframe philanthropy as joyful and meaningful work.

Leadership Imperatives

Leaders who wish to build a culture of philanthropy must:

1. Allocate resources to support fundraising capacity, including staff development and technology.

2. Share transparent fundraising updates on a regular basis.

3. Frame revenue growth as mission-driven, not budget-driven.

4. Practice what they preach through direct engagement with donors.

Ultimately, a culture of philanthropy is about alignment. It synchronizes values and actions, connecting donors with the community and by aligning leadership with the mission. In this type of culture, fundraising is not viewed as a burden or a race for dollars; rather it becomes a shared expression of purpose, built on relationships, trust, and a sense of authentic partnership.

Social Enterprise: Leveraging Market Solutions for Mission Impact

Social enterprise offers nonprofits a way to blend business acumen with social impact. It emphasized the use of income-generating activities to both support the mission and strengthen financial stability. Unlike traditional fundraising, which depends on donations and grants, social enterprises earn revenue by selling products or services, then reinvest those profits back into the organization's work. This strategy that not only brings in funds, but also reinforces the mission through every transaction.

Examples include:

1. A workforce development nonprofit operating a bakery to train and employ participants.

2. An arts organization selling original prints or hosting ticketed performances.

3. A youth-mentoring nonprofit offering leadership retreats to schools for a fee.

Benefits of Social Enterprise

For nonprofit leaders, the appeal of social enterprise lies in its potential to:

1. Reduce dependency on fluctuating philanthropic and government funding.

2. Align income generation with mission delivery.

3. Increase visibility and community engagement.

4. Provide job training or services to constituents as part of the revenue model.

According to the Social Enterprise Alliance (2022), 51% of social enterprises in the U.S. are structured as nonprofits with mission-driven earned income strategies.

Key Considerations for Launch

Social enterprises must be mission-aligned, market-tested, and ethically managed. Leadership should assess:

1. **Feasibility:** Is there a real demand for the product or service?

2. **Mission Fit:** Will the enterprise directly support, not distract from, the mission?

3. **Capacity:** Does the organization have the skills, staff, and systems to operate a business?

4. **Legal Structure:** Will the venture operate under the nonprofit's umbrella or as a separate entity?

A comprehensive business plan that includes pricing, marketing, operations, and risk assessment is essential before launch (Kim & Mauborgne, 2015).

Challenges and Risk Management

Risks include:

1. Diversion of leadership attention from core programs.

2. Financial losses from poorly performing ventures.

3. Brand confusion or public perception that the organization no longer needs donations.

To manage these risks, leaders must establish strong internal controls, monitor performance metrics, and engage the board in oversight. Transparency with donors and stakeholders regarding the purpose and role of the enterprise is key.

Fee-for-Service Models: Contracting with Government and Private Entities

Fee-for-service (FFS) is a funding approach through which non-profits receive payment for the services that they provide, often through contracts or reimbursements from government programs, healthcare providers, or private payers. This model is becoming more common in areas like housing, disability support, behavioral health, and childcare. By getting paid for the work that they already do, nonprofits can create a more stable, predictable revenue stream while continuing to serve their communities.

Examples include:

1. A residential summer camp for adults with disabilities, billing the State Department of Social and Health Services (DSHS).

2. A nonprofit childcare provider receiving state reimbursements for subsidized early learning slots.

3. A senior services agency billing Medicare or Medicaid for case management or transportation services.

4. Characteristics of the FFS Model

FFS revenue typically depends on:

1. Pre-approved contracts, licensing, or provider agreements.

2. Service delivery tied to specific outputs (e.g., hours of care, number of meals).

3. Detailed documentation, billing systems, and regulatory compliance.

This model differs from philanthropy in that it treats the nonprofit as a vendor, delivering measurable services in exchange for payment, often in a competitive procurement environment.

Strategic Value

Properly implemented, fee-for-service models can:

1. Provide reliable, scalable funding.

2. Increase accountability through performance-based contracts.

3. Support mission-critical programs that also meet public mandates.

4. Strengthen partnerships with local and state agencies.

In Washington State, for example, DSHS contracts are a significant funding source for services to vulnerable populations, including adults with intellectual and developmental disabilities, foster youth, and families facing housing instability (Washington State DSHS, 2023).

Operational Implications

Nonprofits using an FFS model must invest in:

1. Billing and reimbursement systems.

2. Compliance protocols and audits.

3. Staff training in service documentation.

4. Cash flow planning (since reimbursements may be delayed).

Failure to meet contract requirements can result in funding clawbacks, fines, or loss of eligibility, making compliance a key leadership concern.

Ethical and Mission Considerations

Leaders must also reflect on:

1. **Equity:** Are services accessible to all, or only to reimbursable clients?

2. **Mission alignment:** Do services meet client needs, or do billing codes shape them?

3. **Sustainability:** What happens if contracts end or rates change?

Like social enterprise, the FFS model must be pursued as part of a balanced revenue strategy, not as a replacement for philanthropy, but as a complement that supports mission delivery through structured, accountable funding streams.

Chapter 3 Summary

Fundraising in the nonprofit sector is not a peripheral task, but a central leadership responsibility that sustains mission impact, builds trust, and fosters long-term organizational health. This chapter has explored a comprehensive spectrum of fundraising models, from traditional grant writing to emerging practices in digital outreach, micro-philanthropy, and social enterprise.

Leaders must recognize that effective fundraising is relational, strategic, and grounded in transparency. Whether engaging a major donor, launching a monthly giving program, or billing a government agency for services, the common thread is alignment: between values and practices, mission and messaging, and community need and resource strategy.

As donor expectations shift and funding becomes more complex, nonprofit leaders need to respond—not by chasing every new trend, but by remaining grounded in strong relationships, a commitment to equity, and a shared sense of purpose across the organization. When fundraising is done well, it does more than keep the lights on: it reflects the organization's integrity, its connection to the community, and its deeper vision for a more just and inclusive future.

Discussion Questions

1. What distinguishes a mission-aligned fundraising strategy from one that is opportunistic or transactional?

2. How can nonprofit leaders ensure that grant-seeking activities do not compromise programmatic autonomy or values?

3. In what ways does your current or prior organization cultivate (or fail to cultivate) a culture of philanthropy?

4. What are the advantages and risks of incorporating fee-for-service models or social enterprise into a nonprofit's revenue portfolio?

5. How can your organization ensure that fundraising practices are inclusive and reflect an equity-centered approach?

6. Reflect on a successful digital or peer-to-peer campaign that you have seen succeed. What made it effective, and what lessons can you apply?

7. What tools and metrics should be in place to assess donor retention and stewardship effectiveness?

Field Markers

1. **Culture of Philanthropy:** An organizational environment in

which fundraising is integrated into the mission, is supported by all staff and board, and is rooted in relational values.

2. **Donor Retention:** Using metrics such as repeat gifts and lifetime value to measure the organization's ability to keep donors engaged and giving over time.

3. **Digital Fundraising:** Using online tools, such as social media, mobile platforms, and crowdfunding sites, to solicit and steward donations.

4. Fee-for-Service Model: A funding approach through which government agencies or private entities pay nonprofits for delivering contracted services.

5. **Micro-Philanthropy:** Engaging many donors to give small amounts, often through monthly giving or mobile campaigns, to create cumulative impact.

6. **Peer-to-Peer Fundraising:** A decentralized fundraising method through which individuals raise funds on behalf of an organization, typically through personal networks.

7. **Social Enterprise:** A mission-driven business operated by a nonprofit to generate earned income while advancing social goals.

8. **Stewardship:** The ethical management of donor relationships through communication, acknowledgment, and demonstration of impact.

9. **Grant Proposal:** A structured request submitted to a foundation, corporation, or government agency to acquire funding for a specific program or initiative.

10. **Community-Centric Fundraising (CCF):** A movement and philosophy that emphasizes equity, collective benefit, and community voice in fundraising practices.

- Chapter 4 -

Program Planning and Development

Program planning is at the heart of nonprofit execution. It is the structured process through which ideas are transformed into interventions and aspirations into outcomes. Effective programs emerge from rigorous inquiry, inclusive design, sound implementation, and continuous reflection. This chapter presents a comprehensive roadmap to help leaders in developing high-impact, mission-aligned programs that are responsive to the communities they serve.

Rather than offering a rigid formula, the chapter equips readers with adaptable tools for a range of contexts, from grassroots initiatives to multi-site operations. Core topics include aligning programs with mission and strategy, conducting equitable needs assessments, using logic models and theory of change, and building sustainability into design from day one.

Readers will also explore participatory planning methods, digital project management tools, risk mitigation strategies, and outcome measurement techniques. A capstone case study brings these elements together in practice, showcasing a program's journey from inception to measurable community benefit.

Learning Objectives

By the end of Chapter 4, readers will be able to:

11. Define the strategic and ethical foundations of nonprofit program planning.

12. Conduct equity-centered community needs assessments.

13. Apply logic models and theory of change to program design.

14. Engage stakeholders using participatory planning methods.

15. Create implementation plans that include staffing, timelines, and project management tools.

16. Develop realistic and mission-aligned program budgets.

17. Identify and mitigate operational, financial, and reputational risks.

18. Design monitoring and evaluation frameworks for continuous improvement.

19. Plan for sustainability beyond the grant cycle.

20. Analyze a comprehensive program case study and extract lessons for practice.

Quick-Glance Map of Chapter 4

Section	Learning Objectives
Understanding Program Planning	Align planning processes with organizational mission and strategic priorities.
Community Needs Assessment	Use data, listening sessions, and equity frameworks to define community needs.
Theory of Change and Logic Models	Visually map program activities to outcomes and impact.
Participatory Design	Collaborate with community, staff, and partners to codesign responsive programs.
Implementation Planning	Plan for staffing, timelines, and tools using modern project management approaches.
Budgeting for Program Success	Develop realistic, grant-aligned, and sustainable budgets.
Risk Management	Identify risks and apply tools to plan for mitigation and legal compliance.

Monitoring and Evaluation	Integrate KPIs and feedback loops for ongoing improvement.
Sustainability Planning	Design programs that last beyond initial funding periods.
Case Study	Analyze a real-world program from idea to impact.

Understanding Program Planning in Context

Program planning is one of the most vital leadership responsibilities in the nonprofit sector. At its heart, program planning consists of transforming vision into action, shaping the day-to-day efforts that bring an organization's mission to life. Far more than being a static plan on paper, effective program planning is a dynamic process of design, implementation, and ongoing refinement. It ensures that services are not only well-organized but also mission-aligned, community-informed, and outcomes-focused.

For today's nonprofit leaders, program planning cannot be treated as a one-time task or a compliance requirement. Instead, it must be approached as a continuous cycle of learning, listening, and adjusting. This mindset helps organizations to remain nimble and grounded in real-world needs, essential attributes as they navigate shifting funding landscapes, demographic changes, and evolving expectations from the communities they serve.

From Traditional to Adaptive Planning

In contrast with traditional planning, adaptive planning creates space for real-time learning, flexibility, and the ability to shift direction when needed. Consider a workforce development nonprofit that, halfway through the year, realized that local employers had shifted their hiring priorities. Rather than adhering rigidly to the original curriculum, the organization adjusted its training modules to match emerging job market needs, demonstrating how responsiveness can turn potential setbacks into strategic pivots. An example of this shift can be seen in a workforce development nonprofit that discovered mid-year that local employers had altered their hiring priorities. With an adaptive planning approach, the nonprofit could retool its training curriculum mid-cycle to emphasize digital competencies without waiting for a new grant cycle or board approval.

This adaptability allows nonprofits to remain relevant, especially in periods of disruption, such as a pandemic or an economic downturn. By planning with the expectation that change is inevitable, leaders foster an environment of innovation and resilience.

Mission Alignment and Strategic Fit

A program's relevance must be continuously evaluated against the organization's mission and long-term strategy. Poorly aligned programs can distract from core priorities, stretch limited resources, and create both internal and external confusion. Leaders must ask themselves not just whether a new program is fundable, but whether it is mission critical. This means assessing the program's alignment with strategic goals, evaluating internal capacity, and anticipating the long-term implications of its adoption.

Consider a food justice organization that receives an opportunity to pursue a grant for mental health services. Even with funding available, leaders must reflect on whether they have the expertise to deliver high-quality care, whether it strengthens or dilutes their identity, and how it may shift organizational focus over time. Mission alignment is both a strategic lens and a safeguard against mission drift.

The Role of Leadership and Governance

Boards of directors and executive leaders are integral to effective program planning. Their role extends beyond approving budgets or evaluating outcomes; they set the tone for strategic coherence, community accountability, and ethical clarity. When governance bodies actively engage with the rationale behind new program ideas by examining their feasibility, potential risks, and alignment with the mission, they offer more than oversight: they offer stewardship.

Effective leaders allocate time for strategic program discussion, ensure resources are deployed appropriately, and foster collaboration across departments. They also create space for experimentation, understanding that innovative ideas often emerge from the intersection of program delivery and community feedback.

Equity and Ethics in Program Planning

Ethical program planning is rooted in social justice. The choices made during the design phase—what problems to address, which communities to serve, whose perspectives are centered—are both moral and strategic decisions. Equity is not simply an add-on, but an essential principle that must inform every stage of planning.

All too often, planning processes unintentionally replicate systems of exclusion. Community engagement is limited to focus groups after the design has been completed, or participation is restricted to those who have the time, language fluency, or transportation needed to attend meetings. Ethical planners address these barriers early and systematically, ensuring that people with lived experience have real influence over program goals, design, and outcomes.

A community health initiative that hires local residents as co-designers and compensates them fairly for their expertise exemplifies this ethical practice. Planning that begins with, and is accountable to, the community results programs that are more trusted, effective, and sustainable.

When program planning is understood as being both strategic and adaptive, nonprofit leaders are positioned to build initiatives that are aligned, inclusive, and impactful. Rather than relying on rigid formulas or chasing funding trends, successful planners approach the work with clarity of purpose, humility, and curiosity. By embedding principles of equity, responsiveness, and mission alignment in planning processes, leaders are better equipped to design programs that truly make a difference.

This foundation sets the stage for the deeper exploration that follows in subsequent sections, from assessing needs to measuring outcomes. In an increasingly complex environment, successful programs are not only well-funded or well-managed, but they are also well-planned.

Assessing and Responding to Community Needs

The best programs begin not with assumptions, but with curiosity. Understanding a community's true needs, and how those needs are experienced by the people who live them, is the first step in designing a successful program.

This section offers a high-level view of the ways in which community needs assessment is integrated with a broader program planning process. While Chapter 5 provides an in-depth guide to the tools, methods, and ethics of needs assessment, here we focus on its strategic role: shaping programs that are mission-aligned, responsive, and rooted.

Why Community Needs Matter

Every nonprofit program exists to solve a problem or meet a need. But how do we know which needs to focus on? And how do we avoid making assumptions based on incomplete data or outdated narratives?

This is the point at which needs assessment enters the picture, helping leaders to ground their program ideas in facts, stories, and lived experience. Done well, it surfaces not only gaps and barriers, but also local assets and strengths. It allows organizations to act with intention rather than instinct, and this makes a measurable difference in both design and impact.

Turning Insight into Strategy

Needs assessment isn't restricted to gathering data. Its real value lies in the use of that data. For nonprofit leaders, this means the application of findings to make strategic decisions about:

1. Which needs your organization is equipped to meet?

2. Where partnerships might strengthen your response?

3. How priorities align with your mission and resources?

When programs are built on a clear understanding of needs, everything from budgeting to evaluation becomes more focused and effective.

Equity Starts Here

The choices that we make during assessments reflect our values. Whom do we listen to? What voices are missing? How are needs defined - and who defines these needs?

Equity-minded leaders pay close attention to these questions, working to ensure that assessments include and honor the perspectives of historically excluded communities. This isn't just a matter of fairness: such focus serves to build programs that communities trust because they see themselves engaged in the process from its inception.

Even simple steps, such as offering translation and interpretation services, holding listening sessions at accessible times, or compensating participants for their time, can shift power in meaningful ways.

A Note for the Road Ahead

This chapter introduces the importance of needs assessment as a core planning tool. But to really do it justice, we dedicate an entire chapter - Chapter 5 - to the deeper methods and ethics of community inquiry. There, you will find guidance on everything from survey design and GIS tools to participatory research and data interpretation.

For now, keep in mind that every strong program begins with a question: "What matters most to the people we serve?" A thoughtful needs assessment helps you to answer that question with clarity, respect, and purpose.

Theory of Change and Logic Models

At the heart of every effective program there exists a clear and coherent theory—an articulation of how specific activities are expected to lead to meaningful outcomes. Theory of Change (ToC) and logic models are two widely used tools that enable nonprofit leaders and practitioners to visualize and communicate this pathway to impact. These frameworks are not merely funder requirements or evaluation tools—they are strategic planning assets that anchor programs in clarity, accountability, and shared understanding.

Understanding Theory of Change

A Theory of Change (ToC) is a narrative or visual explanation of how and why a desired change is expected to happen in a particular context. It traces the logical sequence from inputs and activities to short-, medium-, and long-term outcomes, while making underlying assumptions explicit. Unlike a simple list of goals, ToC invites critical reflection about causality, context, and capacity.

For example, a youth mentoring organization might propose that weekly, structured mentoring sessions (activity) build trusting relationships (short-term outcome), increase self-esteem and academic engagement (medium-term outcomes), and ultimately reduce school dropout rates (long-term impact). The ToC would also note the assumptions: that mentors are effectively trained, that schools provide a supportive environment, and that students are voluntarily engaged.

Developing a Theory of Change involves asking key questions:

1. What is the problem that we are trying to solve?

2. What change do we hope to see, and for whom?

3. What interventions or strategies will lead to that change?

4. What assumptions must hold true for our strategy to succeed?

5. How will we know that we are making progress?

When used collaboratively with program staff, community members, and stakeholders, ToC becomes a unifying tool that sharpens strategy and builds shared purpose.

Logic Models: Visual Roadmaps of Impact

While Theory of Change offers a big-picture rationale, logic models provide a more granular, visual representation of a program's architecture. A typical logic model includes five interconnected components:

1. **Inputs** – Resources needed to implement the program (e.g., funding, staff, facilities)

2. **Activities** – Actions taken or services delivered (e.g., workshops, outreach, training)

3. **Outputs** – Immediate, countable results (e.g., number of clients served, sessions held)

4. **Outcomes** – Changes in knowledge, behavior, or conditions (e.g., increased literacy rates)

5. **Impact** – Long-term, systemic change (e.g., reduced poverty in the target community)

By defining and analyzing these components, logic models help to identify what success looks like at each stage, while ensuring internal alignment. These models are also powerful tools for funders, evaluators, and program staff who need to see how resources translate into results.

From Planning to Evaluation

The value of both ToC and logic models extends far beyond the proposal stage. Each provides a roadmap for implementation, a foundation for performance measurement, and a reference point for mid-course corrections. Programs that regularly revisit and refine these tools, particularly following major shifts in context or outcomes, demonstrate a culture of reflection and continuous improvement.

Moreover, these tools support organizational learning. By contrasting actual outcomes with projected outcomes, leaders can refine strategies, test assumptions, and improve resource allocation. In doing so, the organization becomes more responsive and accountable—to both the community and its mission.

Avoiding Common Pitfalls

Despite their usefulness, ToC and logic models can fall short if treated as bureaucratic exercises. Common challenges include:

1. Oversimplifying complex social change.

2. Using jargon that obscures, rather than clarifies, meaning.

3. Failing to engage frontline staff or community stakeholders in the development process.

To be meaningful, these tools must be developed inclusively, revisited regularly, and connected directly to decisions regarding implementation, staffing, and evaluation.

Theory of Change and logic models serve as roadmaps that help to connect a nonprofit's vision with its day-to-day work - and ultimately, with the impact that it hopes to make. When thoughtfully developed and regularly revisited, these tools do more than organize activities, they bring clarity to complex goals, offer a shared language for communicating with funders and partners, and keep the organization grounded in meaningful outcomes. At their best, they are much more than planning frameworks, they are a visible expression of the nonprofit's commitment to purpose, transparency, and ongoing learning.

Theory of Change vs. Logic Model — What's the Difference?

While often used together, a Theory of Change (ToC) and a Logic Model serve distinctly different purposes in nonprofit planning:

Element	Theory of Change	Logic Model

Purpose	Explains why and how change is expected to happen	Illustrates what activities will lead to specific outputs and outcomes
Scope	Broad, strategic; focuses on long-term goals and causal pathways	Tactical; details program inputs, activities, outputs, and short-term outcomes
Orientation	Backward mapping from the desired impact	Forward mapping from inputs to outcomes
Narrative/ Visual	Often includes a narrative explanation and visual map of change logic	Typically a structured table or flowchart
Use Case	Best for strategic planning, communication with funders, and evaluation frameworks	Best for program management and performance tracking
Strength	Clarifies assumptions and reveals hidden drivers of change	Brings precision and accountability to program execution

Together, these tools help nonprofits align big-picture vision with practical implementation—connecting mission to measurable results.

Participatory Program Design and Stakeholder Engagement

Designing nonprofit programs without community input is comparable to building a bridge without talking to the people who will use it. Participatory program design is more than a best practice, it is a leadership mindset grounded in respect, transparency, and collaboration. By inviting those most affected to help shape the work, leaders ensure that programs are not only more relevant and effective, but also more just. When community members have a voice in decision-making, it builds trust, strengthens relationships, and lays the foundation for long-term impact.

What Is Participatory Design?

Participatory design refers to a set of planning practices through which community members, staff, and partners co-create programs alongside nonprofit leaders. It draws from principles of human-centered design and systems thinking and adapts tools from disciplines such as community organizing, public health, and education.

Participatory design moves beyond consultation. It invites stakeholders into the creative and strategic process of defining problems, generating solutions, and shaping implementation. This participation might take the form of design sprints, co-creation labs, or more grassroots activities such as community story mapping and listening sessions.

Why It Matters

The rationale behind participatory design is both ethical and practical. When people feel heard and respected, they are more likely to support, engage with, and champion programs. And when solutions are developed with deep local knowledge, they are more likely to be contextually relevant and effective.

For example, a health equity nonprofit planning a new maternal care initiative in a multilingual urban neighborhood might begin by recruiting expectant mothers and local health workers to co-lead design sessions. Participants might identify logistical, cultural, or emotional barriers that external planners would miss, such as clinic hours that conflict with work schedules or language used in outreach materials that feels stigmatizing. These insights lead to better design and better results.

Methods and Tools for Inclusive Design

Participatory approaches vary widely depending on context, goals, and community preferences. Common strategies include:

1. **Focus Groups and Town Halls:** Structured conversations that allow participants to share experiences and provide feedback in real time.

2. **Community Advisory Boards:** Ongoing bodies composed of program beneficiaries or representatives who advise and co-create at key decision points.

3. **Design Sprints:** Fast-paced, facilitated sessions in which diverse stakeholders brainstorm, create prototypes, and test ideas over several days.

4. **Story Mapping:** A tool for conveying community history, narratives, and needs through collective storytelling and visual mapping.

No single tool guarantees success; rather, the key is to use methods that are accessible, transparent, and responsive to community preferences. Importantly, inclusion should not be symbolic, it must tangibly influence final decisions.

Power-Sharing and Ethical Considerations

Genuine participatory design asks more of nonprofit leaders than simply inviting people to the table, it requires leaders to share power. This involves listening with humility, being upfront about possibilities, and welcoming disagreement as a form of insight, not resistance. It also means being open to changing course when community feedback uncovers gaps or challenges in the original plan.

Power-sharing also calls for practical support. For example, if a program is reaching out to rural residents, leaders need to consider what is required to make participation feasible, such as offering transportation stipends, providing childcare, or using culturally respectful facilitation methods. Without these supports, the process can unintentionally reinforce the very barriers it intends to break down.

Finally, accountability matters. People who provide their time and ideas deserve to know what their contributions yielded. Clear follow-up - sharing decisions, next steps, and how input was used - builds trust and encourages deeper engagement over time. A simple but often neglected step is closing the loop by communicating to participants the ways in which their contributions shaped the final plan.

Integrating Staff and Partners in Design

Participatory design also strengthens internal culture. When frontline staff are involved in shaping the programs that they will implement, they bring insights from practice that enrich design and increase buy-in. Cross-functional teams that span programs, finance, communications, and evaluation—are more likely to anticipate downstream challenges and co-develop feasible solutions.

Likewise, partners – whether they are funders, schools, or government agencies - can be valuable co-designers if expectations, roles, and values are aligned. The process must be intentionally structured to ensure that the community voice remains centered, and that institutional stakeholders do not dominate the process.

Participatory program design is not a trend—it is a transformative approach rooted in equity, accountability, and humility. By inviting community members, staff, and partners to enter the heart of the planning process, nonprofit leaders can build programs that are more relevant, resilient, and impactful. In a sector dedicated to public good, there is no substitute for shared ownership.

Implementation Planning: Staffing, Timelines, and Tools

Once a program is designed, bringing it to life takes more than good intentions. Meticulous planning, clearly defined roles, and a steady hand are required to manage the details over time. Implementation planning is the point at which vision is translated into action. It turns big-picture goals into coordinated steps that guide teams, allocate resources, and keep the work on track.

For nonprofit leaders, this stage balances practicality with purpose. It means anticipating logistics, budgeting realistically, and preparing for changes along the way, all while adhering to the program's core mission. Strong implementation doesn't just launch a program; it sets the stage for lasting impact.

Building an Implementation Framework

An effective implementation framework weaves together all the pieces needed to bring a program to life: staffing roles, timelines, budgets, and systems for tracking progress. This framework is more than a work plan. It's a living blueprint that helps teams to move from design to delivery with clarity, coordination, and the flexibility to adapt when needed. Leaders begin by identifying major program components, assigning clear responsibilities, and determining the human, financial, and technological resource flows required to sustain each element.

Implementation planning also includes selecting the appropriate tools to monitor progress and enable informed decision-making. These mechanisms can include shared calendars, dashboards, or status check-ins that align internal accountability with external expectations.

Staffing for Success

People are the primary drivers of program success. Designing a staffing plan means more than filling positions—it requires aligning talent with the values and goals of the initiative. Effective staffing structures begin with clearly defined roles and responsibilities. In smaller organizations, one individual may wear multiple hats; in larger programs, functional teams may handle direct service, data tracking, outreach, or evaluation.

For example, a reentry support program might staff case managers to provide individualized coaching, peer mentors to offer lived-experience perspective, and a data coordinator to track outcomes and trends. What connects these roles is not only their function but their alignment with a shared purpose.

Sustained success also depends on supportive onboarding and professional development. Staff need training, not only in technical skills but in cultural competence, trauma-informed care, and mission-driven practices. High-functioning teams are built through intentional supervision, ongoing reflection, and peer learning.

Timelines and Milestone Planning

Timelines are critical to aligning effort and expectation. Effective implementation plans specify when key activities will occur, who is responsible, and how progress will be assessed. Rather than being rigid schedules, timelines should reflect a sequence of deliverables and allow for course correction.

Major phases might include program rollout, participant enrollment, service delivery, and evaluation milestones. Mid-cycle reviews offer opportunities to pause, reflect, and recalibrate. In complex initiatives, Gantt charts and project calendars can help visualize overlapping responsibilities and identify potential bottlenecks before they arise.

Project Management Tools and Technology

Digital project management platforms have become essential infrastructure for nonprofit teams working across functions or geographies. Tools like Asana, Trello, Smartsheet, and Monday.com enable real-time visibility into tasks, deadlines, and progress.

However, the tool is only as effective as the governance behind it. Leaders must clarify who assigns tasks, who monitors deliverables, and how information flows across the team. A shared platform can only support collaboration when paired with communication, documentation, and follow-up norms.

Training is equally important. Staff may vary in digital fluency, and without a shared understanding of how tools fit into the organization's workflow, even robust systems can go underused. Implementation planning should include time to onboard teams onto these platforms and integrate their use into routine operations.

Adaptation and Responsiveness

No plan unfolds exactly as designed. Adaptive implementation acknowledges this reality and embeds flexibility in the process. Regular team check-ins, debriefs after key milestones, and feedback channels from participants all support responsive leadership.

Consider a summer youth program that sees an unexpected enrollment drop. Rather than press forward as planned, leaders might use weekly reflection meetings to identify patterns, gather input from youth and families, and adjust recruitment messaging or service formats. Adaptability is not a sign of weakness, rather, it is the mark of a healthy organization that is willing to listen and evolve.

Programs that encourage candid dialogue, model psychological safety, and respond to frontline feedback are more likely to maintain momentum and foster team cohesion in the face of challenges.

Implementation is the stage at which nonprofit programs are brought to life. It involves more than logistics - it required the translation of intent into action with clarity, coordination, and compassion. Leaders who invest in thoughtful planning, supportive staffing, and adaptive systems position their organizations to deliver high-quality services while building the trust, resilience, and agility needed for long-term impact.

Budgeting for Program Success

A thoughtfully constructed program budget is not simply a spreadsheet—it is an expression of strategic intent. While Chapter 2 explored the broader landscape of nonprofit budgeting, including organizational planning, multi-year forecasting, and financial storytelling, this section focuses more narrowly on budgeting at the program level. It examines how nonprofit leaders ensure that financial plans support programmatic goals, reflect operational realities, and remain responsive throughout the program lifecycle.

The Role of Budgeting in Program Planning

In program planning, the budget plays three key roles. First, it acts as a reality check - can we achieve what we're proposing? Second, it serves as a roadmap for the ways in which resources will be used to bring the program to life. And third, it's a communication tool that shows funders how their support will translate into impact.

By translating program goals into line items, leaders can evaluate whether the organization has the capacity to deliver on its promises, and to determine where additional investment, partnership, or redesign may be necessary. Budgeting also clarifies roles, timelines, and scale, anchoring program plans in the financial context in which they must operate.

This process is not linear. Program design and budgeting usually grow side by side, each shaping, and sometimes limiting, the other. Take, for example, a mental health nonprofit that wants to expand counseling services to rural schools. On paper, the idea might seem straightforward. But as leaders begin building the budget, they realize that hiring licensed clinicians and covering travel costs will stretch resources further than expected. Rather than scrapping the idea, they adapt - perhaps by adding a telehealth option or by partnering with local school districts to share costs. This sort of adaptation isn't a setback; rather, it is a normal part of designing programs that are both ambitious and doable.

Program Budgets and Organizational Strategy

While program budgets must be detailed and accurate, they also need to reflect the organization's larger financial strategy. This includes the proportion of funds allocated to direct service versus administrative support, alignment with funder expectations, and clarity on how costs will be covered once initial grants expire.

Programs that rely heavily on soft money—especially short-term grants—require strong sustainability planning. Leaders must consider whether the program will be integrated into core operations over time, transitioned to earned income, or phased out if future funding is not secured. These conversations should occur during program design, not after launch.

Direct and Indirect Costs

A well-structured program budget distinguishes between direct and indirect costs. Direct costs are those that can be tied specifically to the program, such as staff salaries, supplies, and travel. Indirect costs, often called overhead, cover shared services such as HR, finance, IT, and facility maintenance.

Many funders allow for a percentage of indirect costs, but nonprofit leaders must advocate for full cost recovery. Underbudgeting indirect expenses creates hidden deficits and strains infrastructure. Using transparent allocation models, for example, spreading a portion of administrative salaries across several programs, helps to ensure that costs are shared fairly, and that budgets reflect the true effort it takes to run the organization. This is a practical approach to promote both accuracy and equity in resource planning.

In-Kind Contributions and Match Requirements

Some programs benefit from, or require, in-kind contributions, such as volunteer hours, donated space, or pro bono services. These contributions should be documented and appropriately valued in the budget. In competitive grant environments, demonstrating community investment through in-kind support can strengthen applications and help in meeting match requirements.

Nonprofits should develop internal systems to consistently track these contributions. Such tracking not only supports compliance, but provides a fuller picture of program resources, enhancing both transparency and storytelling.

Scenario Planning and Budget Flexibility

Even the most meticulous program budgets require adaptability. Changes in participant volume, staffing needs, or vendor pricing can create variance. Leaders should incorporate modest contingency lines and revisit program budgets quarterly to make any needed adjustments.

Scenario planning - introduced in Chapter 2 - can also be applied at the program level. For instance, if a summer camp faces enrollment uncertainty, budget scenarios might model outcomes for 50, 75, or 100 participants. Each scenario would adjust staffing, supply costs, and revenue projections in accordance with enrollment, enabling faster, data-informed decisions.

Program budgeting involves more than crunching numbers: it is a blend of technical skill and strategic thinking. A strong budget helps to ensure that a program is not only well-designed, but also doable with the available resources, supported by the appropriate staff and systems, and aligned with the bigger picture of the organization's mission.

When leaders approach budgeting, not as an afterthought, but as a core part of program planning, they are better equipped to build programs that are grounded, realistic, and enduring. It is this form of thoughtful planning that allows nonprofits to deliver meaningful results while remaining true to their values and commitments.

Risk Management in Program Design

Risk is an inherent part of program planning and execution. Whether it stems from funding volatility, staffing challenges, data privacy concerns, or community backlash, risk cannot be eliminated—but it can be anticipated, assessed, and mitigated. Effective nonprofit leaders embed risk management in the earliest stages of program design, ensuring that uncertainty does not derail mission delivery or erode stakeholder trust.

Understanding Program Risk

Program risks fall into several broad categories: financial, operational, legal, reputational, and strategic. Financial risks can include underperforming fundraising campaigns or overreliance on a single grant. Operational risks can arise from supply chain interruptions, staff turnover, or technology failures. Legal and compliance risks can involve licensing, insurance coverage, data security regulations, or service delivery standards. Reputational risk often stems from communication missteps, or from unintended harm to clients and communities.

Strategic risk—perhaps the most underappreciated category— occurs when a program's design is misaligned with the organization's core mission, or when mission drift results from pursuing poorly suited funding opportunities.

Integrating Risk Analysis into Planning

Risk management is not a separate process; rather it is an integral component of responsible planning. During program design, nonprofit leaders should engage in structured risk assessments that expose potential challenges before they escalate.

Tools such as SWOT (Strengths, Weaknesses, Opportunities, Threats) analysis or risk matrices can help to identify vulnerabilities and categorize them by likelihood and impact. These tools do not require elaborate models; rather, they depend on honest discussion, cross-functional insight, and a commitment to naming risks without stigma.

For example, a program that is launching services in a new community might identify high staff turnover as a moderate-likelihood, high-impact risk. In response, the plan could incorporate peer support models, invest in robust onboarding, or budget for temporary staffing services.

SWOT Analysis for a Community Action Agency

Strengths	Weaknesses
Deep community trust and name recognition built over 50+ years	Limited affordable housing stock constrains program outcomes
Diverse funding portfolio (CSBG, HUD, USDA, local philanthropy)	Heavy reliance on grant cycles for core programs
Strong service integration model (housing, energy, food, health navigation)	Aging infrastructure in community centers and facilities
Experienced, mission-driven staff and volunteers	Gaps in digital systems and data integration across departments
Tripartite governance structure that includes low-income representation	Staff retention challenges due to competitive salaries in private sector

Opportunities	Threats
Expand Meals on Wheels as a social enterprise (sliding scale + earned income)	Rising inflation and cost of living outpacing client income supports
Strengthen rural digital access via broadband equity partnerships	Unpredictable federal and state budget cycles impacting service continuity
Deepen collaboration with tribal governments and rural health providers	Extreme weather events increasing demand on already stretched resources
Use client voice tools (e.g., 360° surveys, story mapping) to enhance design	Burnout among staff due to rising caseloads and emotional labor
Engage younger volunteers through digital outreach and AmeriCorps programs	Housing development constraints due to zoning and NIMBYism in key regions

Proactive Mitigation and Scenario Planning

Once risks have been identified, the next step is to develop mitigation strategies. These should be both preventive and responsive. For instance, preventive actions might include diversifying revenue sources, cross-training staff, or investing in secure data infrastructure. Responsive plans could include communication protocols for service disruptions or pre-negotiated vendor agreements in case of delays.

Scenario planning, introduced in Chapter 2, becomes especially valuable at this stage. Modeling "what if" situations, such as a 20% budget cut or the sudden loss of a major community partner, enables organizations to identify trigger points and response pathways before a crisis occurs.

Compliance, Insurance, and Legal Safeguards

Nonprofits also have formal obligations tied to compliance and liability. Programs involving vulnerable populations, data collection, medical services, or transportation often require licensing, background checks, data protection measures, and tailored insurance coverage. These must be factored into the program budget and timeline.

Consulting with legal counsel or insurance providers early in the planning phase ensures that requirements are not overlooked. In some cases, insurance riders or waivers may be needed to cover new risks introduced by a pilot program or facility expansion.

Culture and Communication of Risk

Risk management is as much about organizational culture as it is about checklists. Leaders must cultivate an environment in which risks can be identified and discussed without fear, staff feel empowered to express concerns, and failures are used as learning opportunities.

Clear internal communication channels are essential. Program teams should regularly discuss emerging issues in team meetings, and executive leadership should reinforce the message that identifying risk is a sign of foresight, not failure.

Externally, the ways in which organizations communicate about risk during a crisis also shapes reputation. Transparency, timeliness, and empathy are key. An organization that acknowledges a misstep, explains corrective action, and invites feedback will often strengthen trust, rather than damaging it.

Risk management in program design is a proactive leadership practice that protects organizational integrity and strengthens long-term resilience. Through early risk assessment, contingency planning, and the fostering of open dialogue, nonprofit leaders can reduce surprises and improve outcomes. In a sector defined by complexity and change, readiness is not optional—it is a responsibility.

Monitoring, Evaluation, and Continuous Improvement

Monitoring and evaluation (M&E) are not simply tools for funder reporting—they are leadership practices that drive learning, accountability, and strategic refinement. When embedded from the outset, M&E allows organizations to measure what matters, track their progress toward impact, and improve performance over time. In an era in which transparency and outcomes matter more than ever, nonprofit leaders must approach M&E as an essential component of program design, not as an afterthought.

The Purpose of M&E in Nonprofit Programs

At its core, M&E is about determining whether a program is working, for whom, and under what conditions. Monitoring refers to the ongoing tracking of program activities and outputs, while evaluation assesses the outcomes and longer-term impacts. Together, M&E enables leaders to answer the questions: Are we doing what we said we would do? Are we achieving the intended results? How can we improve?

M&E also plays a key role in stakeholder communication. Donors, community members, and partners want to understand how resources are being used and what changes are occurring as a result. An effective M&E framework builds credibility by linking data to decision-making and storytelling.

Building an M&E Framework

Designing an M&E framework begins with clarifying program goals and identifying measurable indicators. These should be SMART—Specific, Measurable, Achievable, Relevant, and Time-bound. Indicators should reflect both outputs (what was delivered) and outcomes (what changed as a result).

For example, a literacy program might track the number of tutoring sessions provided (output) as well as improvements in student reading levels (outcome). Long-term impact might include graduation rates or college enrollment trends.

Data collection methods should be tailored to the context and include both quantitative (e.g., surveys, attendance records) and qualitative (e.g., interviews, focus groups, testimonials) approaches. Leaders must ensure that data systems are user-friendly, ethical, and secure, especially when working with vulnerable populations.

Embedding Feedback Loops

Evaluation is not only about retrospective analysis but also reflects a process of continuous learning. High-performing nonprofits establish regular feedback loops through which data is reviewed, discussed, and used to make real-time adjustments. Such feedback loops could include monthly program dashboards, quarterly reflection meetings, or periodic beneficiary listening sessions.

Frontline staff should be engaged in this process, not just as data collectors, but as co-interpreters of results. Their insights often reveal the "why" behind the numbers leading to practical improvements. Organizations that value feedback as a tool for learning - not judgment - tend to be more adaptive and innovative.

Tying M&E to Organizational Strategy

Monitoring and evaluation should be closely aligned with the organization's theory of change and strategic plan. Logic models, discussed in Section 4.3, provide a natural foundation for selecting indicators and identifying points of measurement. Data from M&E activities can also inform resource allocation, board decision-making, and strategic planning cycles.

Moreover, tying M&E to equity goals is increasingly recognized as best practice. This involves disaggregating data by race, gender, geography, or other relevant demographics to understand who is benefiting - and who is not. It also means communities engage in defining what success looks like and how it should be measured.

Challenges and Opportunities

Despite its importance, many nonprofits struggle with M&E due to limited staff capacity, outdated systems, or fear of negative results. Leaders must cultivate a culture in which learning is prioritized over perfection, and transparency is viewed as a strength.

Investing in appropriate tools, such as Salesforce Nonprofit Cloud, Apricot by Bonterra, or low-cost survey platforms like Google Forms, can reduce administrative burden. Partnerships with academic institutions or volunteer data analysts may also help to build capacity.

The key is to start with what is meaningful and manageable. A simple, well-used dashboard often delivers more value than a complex system that may discourage staff engagement.

When approached thoughtfully, monitoring and evaluation empower nonprofit leaders to steer programs toward greater relevance, effectiveness, and equity. By embedding feedback, measuring what matters, and acting on insights, organizations transform M&E from a compliance exercise into a strategic advantage. In the cycle of planning, doing, learning, and improving, evaluation is the link that makes growth possible.

Sustainability Planning and Post-Grant Continuity

Sustainability in program planning is about much more than financial survival - it enables programs to maintain relevance, value, and impact over time. Too often, nonprofits focus on securing initial funding and launching services without developing an equally robust plan for what happens after the grant ends. A sustainability mindset shifts the focus from temporary intervention to long-term contribution, prompting leaders to ask: How will this program continue to deliver impact when initial funding runs out?

Why Sustainability Planning Matters

Sustainability planning is about foresight and intentionality. It implements strategic decision-making early in the program design process to extend the program's life cycle and deepen its long-term viability. This planning includes financial models, partnership development, community ownership, and leadership continuity.

Without such planning, nonprofits risk launching promising programs that fade once start-up funds are exhausted, eroding community trust and organizational credibility. Programs with strong sustainability plans are more likely to attract follow-on funding, retain staff, and build momentum over time.

Designing for Continuity

Sustainable programs are built with an eye toward adaptability, scalability, and relevance. Leaders must assess which aspects of the program can be integrated into core operations, spun off into partnerships, transitioned to earned income models, or adopted by community stakeholders.

For instance, a youth mentorship program originally funded by a three-year foundation grant might continue beyond the grant period by integrating volunteer support from local colleges, leveraging in-kind contributions from community centers, and incorporating a fee-for-service training model for school districts.

Key questions to consider during planning include:

1. What are the core elements of the program that must be preserved?
2. What internal capacity (staff, systems, leadership) is needed to sustain these elements?
3. Who are the potential partners or funders who align with the long-term vision?
4. What infrastructure (data systems, communications, facilities) is necessary to support continuity?

Diversified Revenue and Strategic Partnerships

While grant funding may provide the initial runway, long-term sustainability often requires a more diversified portfolio. This portfolio may include individual donor cultivation, corporate sponsorships, earned income strategies, or public contracts. Not all sources are appropriate for every program, but leaders should explore revenue alignment as part of strategic planning, rather than as a crisis response.

Partnerships can also prove to be powerful vehicles for sustainability. Collaborating with schools, health agencies, or grassroots organizations can reduce duplication, share infrastructure, and embed programs within systems that already serve the target population. Formalizing partnerships through MOUs or shared outcomes agreements helps protect program fidelity over time.

Institutional Knowledge and Succession

Programs also require human continuity. Sustainability planning should include knowledge transfer practices to preserve institutional memory. This might involve developing standard operating procedures, onboarding guides, or shared documentation systems.

Leadership succession planning is equally important. Programs that hinge on a charismatic founder or a single staff member are vulnerable. By building distributed leadership and codifying decision-making processes, organizations reduce dependency and promote resilience.

Telling the Story of Impact

As discussed in Chapter 2, financial storytelling plays a crucial role in sustaining funding and community support. Programs with clear, compelling narratives of impact that are supported by data and testimonials are more likely to attract renewed investment.

Sharing stories of transformation, quantifying outcomes, and demonstrating return on investment helps funders, donors, and the broader public to understand why a program matters and why it deserves continued support.

Sustainability is not the final chapter of a program—it is an integral part of the design process. Through early planning for financial, operational, and leadership continuity, nonprofit leaders position their programs to survive and thrive beyond the initial grant cycle. This forward-thinking approach signals a commitment to long-term impact, organizational integrity, and community trust.

Here are four practical examples of story mapping, each illustrating different goals and methods:

1. Community Health Access Story Map

1. **Setting:** A rural public health nonprofit in Appalachia

2. **Use Case:** Understanding barriers to accessing preventative healthcare

3. **Method:**Participants were invited to create personal journey maps showing their experience seeking healthcare—where they started, what obstacles they encountered (e.g., transportation, hours of operation, lack of childcare), and how they resolved or abandoned the effort.

Outcomes:

1. Identified that bus routes didn't align with clinic hours.

2. Revealed fears about stigma when seeking mental health care.

3. Informed a new partnership between clinics and mobile health vans.

2. Housing Insecurity Narrative Map

1. **Setting:** Urban homelessness prevention coalition

2. **Use Case:** Designing wraparound support services for housing-vulnerable populations

3. **Method:**Using a large mural board and timeline, individuals experiencing housing instability added sticky notes, photos,

or short stories to illustrate their housing journey - job loss, eviction, shelter use, and interactions with agencies.

Outcomes:

1. Visualized cyclical patterns of temporary stability and crisis.

2. Identified agencies offering redundant services, marred by gaps in mental health and legal aid.

3. Inspired development of a co-located services hub.

3. Youth Engagement Map in Underserved Neighborhoods

1. **Setting:** Youth development nonprofit working in a marginalized neighborhood.

2. **Use Case:** Mapping safe and unsafe community spaces from teens' perspectives.

3. **Method:** Youth were given neighborhood maps and markers to note spaces in which they felt safe, included, or inspired, and those in which they felt excluded, harassed, or ignored. This exercise was followed by group discussion and digital mapping.

Outcomes:

1. Park labeled "unsafe" despite being renovated (due to police surveillance).

2. Informal gathering space behind the library noted as inclusive and creative.

3. Led to youth-led design of a new recreation program and library annex.

4. Refugee Resettlement and Service Navigation

1. **Setting:** A refugee resettlement agency supporting Afghan families

2. **Use Case:** Improving service orientation and case management.

3. **Method:** Caseworkers invited families to draw their journey from arrival to current stability, illustrating what helped, what was confusing, and where they felt unsupported. Translators, interpreters, and community navigators facilitated.

Outcomes:

1. Highlighted the importance of early access to translated housing documents.

2. Families emphasized the emotional support of cultural mentors more than financial aid.

3. Agency modified its intake flow to frontload trust-building and orientation.

How to Use Story Mapping in Your Work

1. **Supplies:** Poster boards, timelines, maps, sticky notes, markers, or digital tools like Miro or StoryMapJS.

2. **Prompts:** "What was your journey like?", "Where did you feel stuck?", "What helped you move forward?"

3. **Facilitation:** Ensure psychological safety, language access, and trauma-informed methods.

4. **Follow-up:** Synthesize findings and share how input informed decisions—close the feedback loop.

Case Study:
A Model Program from Design to Impact

To illustrate the principles of strategic program planning in action, this case study follows the development of "Pathways to Opportunity," a workforce development initiative launched by a mid-sized community-based nonprofit serving a post-industrial city in the Midwest. The program was designed to support unemployed and underemployed adults, especially those adversely affected by incarceration, housing instability, or long-term disconnection from the workforce.

Identifying the Need

The program originated from a community needs assessment that combined quantitative labor market data with qualitative insights from focus groups. The findings revealed that while local employers reported a shortage of skilled workers, residents cited barriers such as lack of transportation, limited digital literacy, and histories of justice involvement as major obstacles to employment. A planning team of staff, board members, and community stakeholders used this data to draft a Theory of Change that linked skills training, case management, and employer partnerships to long-term economic mobility.

Design and Development

Through a participatory design process, the team co-designed a three-part intervention: soft skills and digital literacy workshops, industry-recognized certification programs in manufacturing and healthcare, and job placement support. Local employers were engaged early through a roundtable structure, ensuring that the program addressed actual hiring needs. The logic model connected inputs (funding, staff, curriculum) to outputs (training hours, job placements) and projected outcomes (employment retention, wage growth).

Implementation Planning

The team developed an 18-month implementation plan using Smartsheet to coordinate timelines, onboarding, and partner contributions. Program staff were recruited with lived experience, including returning citizens, to reflect the population being served. The leadership team built contingency plans for technology challenges and participant drop-off, embedding adaptive strategies from the outset.

Budgeting and Funding

An initial pilot budget of $450,000 was funded through a mix of local foundation grants and a city workforce development contract. The program budget clearly delineated direct and indirect costs, including shared administrative support. In-kind contributions from employer partners, including training space and equipment, reduced facility overhead.

To support sustainability, the nonprofit launched a parallel donor campaign and explored social enterprise opportunities to monetize the digital literacy curriculum with other community-based organizations.

Monitoring and Evaluation

The M&E framework included both formative and summative components. Data dashboards tracked enrollment, completion rates, and job placement, while quarterly learning sessions brought together staff, partners, and participants to contemplate challenges and improvements. Feedback led to the addition of evening classes, a new childcare partnership, and culturally specific support groups.

Sustainability and Scale

By its second year, the program had placed 78% of participants in full-time employment. A compelling combination of participant testimonials and ROI analysis (every $1 invested generated $2.80 in public benefit through reduced recidivism and increased earnings) helped to secure multi-year funding from a regional philanthropic collaborative. The nonprofit is now developing replication guides to scale the model to nearby communities.

"Pathways to Opportunity" exemplifies how effective program planning moves from vision to measurable impact. It demonstrates the value of community voice, strategic alignment, adaptive design, and sustainability thinking. Above all, it underscores the power of a well-executed program to shift both individual lives and broader systems.

Discussion Questions

1. **Mission Alignment:** How can nonprofit leaders determine whether a new program idea aligns with their organization's mission and strategic goals? Share an example of a potential program that could lead to mission drift if not carefully evaluated.

2. **Equity in Needs Assessment:** What are the ethical considerations in designing and conducting a community needs assessment? How can leaders ensure that marginalized voices are centered and heard?

3. **Theory of Change vs. Logic Models:** Compare and contrast the utility of a Theory of Change and a logic model in program design. In what situations might one tool be more effective than the other?

4. **Participatory Design Challenges:** What are common barriers to effective participatory design, and how can nonprofits overcome these challenges to ensure authentic stakeholder engagement?

5. **Adaptive Implementation:** Share a scenario where a nonprofit had to modify its implementation plan mid-cycle. What strategies supported the adaptation, and what were the lessons learned?

6. **Budget Realism and Flexibility:** How can program leaders balance aspirational goals with financial constraints when building a budget? Discuss the role of contingency planning and scenario modeling.

7. **Risk Management Culture:** How can nonprofit leaders build an organizational culture that supports proactive risk management and open communication about uncertainty?

8. **Data-Informed Learning:** What are the key components of a strong monitoring and evaluation framework? How can data be used not only for compliance but for organizational learning and storytelling?

9. **Sustainability Thinking:** What strategies can nonprofits use to sustain program impact after the initial funding ends? Discuss the benefits and challenges of partnership-based sustainability models.

10. **Case Study Reflection:** Based on the "Pathways to Opportunity" case study, which aspects of the planning and development process were most critical to the program's long-term success?

Field Markers

1. **Adaptive Planning:** A flexible approach to program development that allows for continuous learning and course correction based on new information or changing conditions.

2. **Asset Mapping:** A participatory process used to identify the strengths, resources, and capacities of individuals and communities as part of needs assessments.

3. **Community Needs Assessment:** A systematic process for identifying and analyzing the needs, assets, and priorities of

a community to inform program development.

4. **Equity-Centered Assessment:** An inclusive approach to data collection and analysis that prioritizes the voices and experiences of historically marginalized populations.

5. **Implementation Plan:** A strategic blueprint outlining the steps, staffing, timeline, and resources required to operationalize a program.

6. **In-Kind Contributions:** Non-cash resources provided to an organization, such as volunteer time, donated goods, or pro bono services, often documented for matching or reporting purposes.

7. **Logic Model:** A visual tool that outlines the relationships among a program's inputs, activities, outputs, outcomes, and long-term impact.

8. **Monitoring and Evaluation (M&E):** Systems and processes used to track program performance, assess outcomes, and inform decision-making and continuous improvement.

9. **Participatory Design:** A collaborative planning method that actively involves community members, staff, and other stakeholders in the creation and refinement of programs.

10. **Risk Management:** The identification, assessment, and mitigation of potential threats to a program's success, including financial, legal, operational, and reputational risks.

11. **Scenario Planning:** A strategic tool that explores multiple future possibilities to help organizations prepare for uncertainties and plan flexible responses.

12. **Sustainability Planning:** The process of ensuring that a program can continue to deliver value and impact beyond initial funding, often through diversified revenue, partnerships, and institutional integration.

13. **Theory of Change (ToC):** A comprehensive framework

that articulates how and why a desired change is expected to happen within a specific context, identifying the causal pathways from actions to outcomes.

- Chapter 5 -

Assessing Community Needs

Effective nonprofit leaders begin, not with assumptions, but with inquiry. Community needs assessments offer a structured, equity-informed approach to understanding local conditions, identifying service gaps, and prioritizing resources. Far from being a procedural exercise, needs assessment is a strategic leadership function that shapes programming, deepens relationships, and positions the organization as an accountable, trusted community partner.

As funders demand more data-driven planning and as communities call for authentic engagement, the methods and mindset behind needs assessments are evolving. This chapter explores techniques and tools, both traditional and emergent, that empower organizations to assess community needs with rigor, humility, and justice at their focus.

Learning Objectives

By the end of Chapter 5, readers will be able to:

1. Differentiate among types of community needs and understand their implications for nonprofit planning.

2. Design an inclusive and ethically grounded needs assessment strategy.

3. Use qualitative and quantitative tools to gather and analyze community data.

4. Conduct equity-centered assessments that avoid deficit framing and promote community voice.

5. Apply participatory methods that engage community members as co-researchers.

6. Evaluate and use tech tools such as GIS and online survey plat-

forms to support assessment.

7. Translate assessment findings into actionable, strategic priorities that inform programs and policy.

Quick-Glance Map of Chapter 5: Assessing Community Needs

Section	Learning Objective
Understanding Community Needs	Define and categorize community needs in context.
Designing the Assessment Approach	Strategically design assessments with purpose, scope, and scale.
Data Collection Methods and Tools	Apply mixed-method strategies for gathering actionable information.
Equity-Centered Practices	Avoid bias and frame assessments through a justice-informed lens.
Participatory Methods	Engage community members in co-design and interpretation.
Data Analysis and Interpretation	Translate complex data into meaningful, accurate insights.
From Assessment to Action	Move from findings to program, advocacy, and resource strategy.
Case Study	Learn from a real-world example of participatory assessment.

Understanding Community Needs

Before launching a program or proposing a new initiative, non-profit leaders must pause to ask: What does the community truly need? Answering that question requires clarity about what "need" actually means and the ways in which it differs from related concepts, such as demand, preference, or resource scarcity. This section lays the foundation for the rest of the chapter by exploring the types of needs that assessments typically seek to identify as well as the ethical considerations that shape the definition of needs.

Types of Community Needs

Needs can be categorized in several ways:

1. **Expressed needs** are those communicated directly by individuals—what people say they need, often observable through behaviors such as service use or advocacy (Bradshaw, 1972).

2. **Felt needs** refer to personal perceptions of unmet need, even when those needs are not vocalized. These can be uncovered through interviews or listening sessions.

3. **Normative needs** are based on expert standards or benchmarks. For example, if a city has fewer than the recommended number of mental health professionals per capita, that shortfall reflects a normative need.

4. **Comparative needs** emerge from analyzing differences across populations or geographies. If one neighborhood has significantly fewer after-school programs than a demographically similar area, a comparative need exists.

Understanding these categories helps leaders to design more responsive assessments and interpret results in a more nuanced manner.

The Difference Between Needs and Wants

While community members are the best judges of their lived experience, not every desire reflects a true "need" in a service context. Leaders must be cautious not to dismiss community input even as they remain disciplined in distinguishing between structural barriers (e.g., lack of transportation access) and program preferences (e.g., preferred class times). The goal is to prioritize actions that advance equity and wellbeing at scale, without invalidating anyone's voice. (Kettner, Moroney, & Martin, 2017).

From Deficit Framing to Asset Awareness

Needs assessments have often focused narrowly on gaps, problems, or deficits. Although identifying barriers is essential, overemphasizing deficits can stigmatize communities and obscure local strengths. Today's best practices encourage a dual focus: identifying challenges while also recognizing assets—such as social networks, cultural practices, or informal support systems—that are vital to community resilience (McKnight & Kretzmann, 1996).

For instance, an assessment in a low-income immigrant neighborhood might reveal food insecurity alongside strong networks of mutual aid and culturally specific food knowledge. A strengths-based assessment would highlight both.

The Ethics of Defining Need

Every decision in a needs assessment—from whose voice is prioritized to which issues are framed as urgent—has ethical implications. Assessments must be designed with care to avoid reinforcing power imbalances, marginalizing certain groups, or imposing external definitions of what matters.

Leaders should reflect on questions such as:

1. Who is framing the inquiry, and with what assumptions?

2. Whose needs are being assessed, and who gets to validate them?

3. Are the findings being used to uplift communities or simply

to fulfill funding requirements?

These considerations ensure that the assessment process itself aligns with the values of equity, transparency, and shared accountability (Coulton, Chan, & Mikelbank, 2011).

Understanding the types of needs, and the frameworks used to define them, is the first step in designing effective and ethical assessments. By balancing rigor with empathy, nonprofit leaders can build a clearer picture of community priorities, laying the foundation for inclusive, actionable strategies.

Designing the Assessment Approach

Once nonprofit leaders understand the different types of community needs, and the ethical responsibilities that come with identifying them, the next step is to design an assessment strategy that reflects their organization's unique mission, capacity, and context. An effective approach is not one-size-fits-all: it must be both intentional and practical. It should build on existing relationships and resources while actively engaging those whom the organization seeks to serve. When thoughtfully constructed, a needs assessment becomes more than an exercise in data collection, it becomes a tool for reflection, trust-building, and strategic alignment. When assessments are transparently designed and carried out with flexibility, the results are more likely to be trusted, useful, and ready to guide real-world decisions.

Clarifying the Purpose of the Assessment

Needs assessments are not one-size-fits-all. The purpose behind the assessment influences every subsequent decision, ranging from data collection methods to stakeholder engagement. Common objectives include:

1. **Strategic planning:** Identifying priorities for long-term organizational direction.

2. **Program design or refinement:** Informing the creation of new services or adjusting existing ones.

3. **Grant or contract compliance:** Meeting funder mandates for documented community need.

4. **Advocacy and systems change:** Generating data to support policy influence or systems-level reform.

Articulating the "why" helps to prevent scope drift, grounding the process in a shared sense of intent (Netting, O'Connor, & Fauri, 2008).

Determining Scope and Scale

The scale of a needs assessment should match its purpose and available resources. A large-scale, citywide assessment might involve extensive data collection, stakeholder interviews, and geospatial analysis, while a program-specific assessment might focus on a single population or neighborhood. Leaders must consider both the breadth of information required and the depth of insight needed to make confident decisions.

Questions to clarify scope include:

1. What geographic or demographic boundaries define our target population?

2. Are we assessing for a single program, an entire organization, or a broader system?

3. How much time and funding do we have to complete this work?

Choosing a Methodological Framework

Methodological decisions should align with the purpose and scope, while centering equity and rigor. In practice, the most effective nonprofit assessments blend both numbers and stories. Surveys and public datasets provide a broad illustration of trends and patterns, while tools such as interviews, focus groups, and story circles introduce and incorporate the voices and lived experiences behind the data. Together, they offer a fuller, more meaningful understanding of community needs.

Some frameworks to consider:

1. **PRECEDE-PROCEED model**: Emphasizes social, epidemiological, and behavioral assessments in health-focused contexts. (Green & Kreuter, 2005)

2. **Asset-Based Community Development (ABCD)**: Focuses on strengths, capacities, and social capital, rather than deficits. (Kretzmann & McKnight, 1993)

3. **Participatory Action Research (PAR)**: Engages community members as co-investigators throughout the assessment process.

Each approach has its own strengths and limitations. The key is to choose a framework that resonates with the organization's values, capacity, and goals.

Addressing Constraints and Readiness

Even the most well-designed assessment strategy must account for practical constraints, including staffing limitations, community fatigue from over-surveying, political sensitivities, and digital divides that affect access to online tools. Leaders must assess their organization's readiness for undertaking a needs assessment by addressing questions of whether there is buy-in from leadership, alignment with strategic priorities, and sufficient time to engage stakeholders meaningfully.

Risk mitigation strategies might include:

1. Phasing the assessment into stages.

2. Partnering with academic institutions or peer organizations.

3. Building on existing data to reduce burden on participants.

Designing a community needs assessment means striking a balance between ambition and feasibility, and between asking the right questions while remaining humble in the process. When nonprofit leaders take the time to clarify their purpose, define a manageable scope, choose the correct approach, and plan for real-world challenges, they create a foundation for work that is ethical, thorough, and meaningful to the communities that they serve.

Data Collection Methods and Tools

Once the framework is set, the next step is choosing the right tools to gather information that truly matters. This process involves more than choosing between surveys or interviews: it requires careful thought about how to listen to the community in ways that reflect its members' real experiences, while supporting the organization's goals. The methods that are chosen shape what is learned and how useful it will be in driving meaningful change. Nonprofit leaders must strike a balance between methodological rigor, cultural relevance, and logistical practicality. For instance, while statistically robust surveys can offer breadth, focus groups or community listening sessions may yield deeper, context-rich insights (Gupta, Fawcett, & Valdovinos, 2022).

Importantly, the data collection process should elevate and amplify the community voice, rather than simply extracting information for institutional use. When intentionally designed, these methods can inform responsive programs, shape advocacy agendas, and direct philanthropic or governmental investment toward areas of highest need (Center for Community Health and Development, 2023). In this way, data becomes a vehicle for both evaluation and equity.

Quantitative Methods: Breadth and Generalizability

Quantitative data offers measurable, broadly applicable insights that often are necessary for funders, policymakers, and strategic planning. Surveys, administrative data, and public datasets provide structured information that can be analyzed at scale.

Surveys are among the most common tools. These can be deployed online, by phone, or in person. Platforms like SurveyMonkey, Qualtrics, and Google Forms offer customizable templates, branching logic, and data export functions. Well-designed surveys should include clear, concise language and facilitate both closed- and open-ended responses (Dillman, Smyth, & Christian, 2014).

Secondary data, such as U.S. Census Bureau data, American Community Survey (ACS), CDC health indicators, and local administrative data (e.g., school performance, housing statistics) provide a macro-level view. This data helps validate trends observed in smaller samples or qualitative research.

GIS Mapping tools, such as ESRI or Social Explorer, can visualize geographic disparities and overlay multiple data layers (e.g. poverty rates, housing conditions, or public transit access), supporting place-based strategies.

Qualitative Methods: Depth and Context

Qualitative data adds the "why" behind the numbers. Through open-ended dialogue, community members share narratives, perceptions, and priorities that may be missed when using standardized instruments.

Interviews provide deep, individualized insight and are ideal for understanding stakeholder experiences, decision-making processes, or barriers to service. Semi-structured formats allow for consistent comparison while encouraging organic exploration.

Focus groups enable group-level reflection, generating rich discussion among individuals with shared or differing perspectives. Skilled facilitation is essential to ensure that all voices are heard and dominant speakers do not distort the dialogue (Krueger & Casey, 2015).

Community listening sessions are informal, inclusive forums designed to surface grassroots concerns. These sessions are especially valuable in marginalized communities where trust in institutions may be low.

Choosing the Right Tool:
Qualitative vs. Quantitative

To make informed decisions, nonprofit leaders must understand the strengths and limitations of both qualitative and quantitative methods. Use this comparison as a guide when planning needs assessments, program evaluations, or stakeholder engagement efforts.

Dimension	Qualitative	Quantitative
Purpose	Understand "why" and "how" people experience an issue	Measure "how many," "how often," and "to what extent"
Data Type	Text, interviews, observations, open-ended responses	Numbers, statistics, closed-ended surveys
Tools	Focus groups, interviews, field notes	Surveys, tests, administrative data
Analysis	Thematic coding, narrative synthesis	Statistical models, trends, inferential tests
Sample	Small, non-random, purposefully selected	Large, random or representative
Strengths	Rich detail, contextual understanding, stakeholder voice	Generalizable, objective, scalable
Limitations	May lack generalizability, more subjective	Can overlook nuance or individual stories
Use in Practice	Community listening sessions, program design, case studies	Dashboards, performance tracking, outcome evaluation
Key Questions	Why? How? What's the experience?	How much? How often? What's the result?
Output Format	Stories, quotes, visual maps	Graphs, charts, numeric summaries

Leadership Tip: The most effective nonprofit evaluations often blend both approaches. A mixed-methods strategy captures the depth of lived experience and the clarity of measurable results.

Mixed-Method Approaches and Triangulation

Most needs assessments benefit from a mixed-method approach. By combining surveys, administrative data, and direct engagement with community members, organizations can triangulate findings and increase credibility.

For example, if quantitative data shows low rates of prenatal care use in a specific ZIP code, and interviews with mothers reveal barriers such as clinic hours or lack of childcare, the resulting recommendations will be more comprehensive and grounded.

Technology Tools and Digital Considerations

Digital tools can facilitate information gathering, especially when communities are spread out or time is limited. But it's important to remember that not everyone has equal access to technology. Online surveys and virtual interviews can exclude people who lack reliable internet, such as elders, rural residents, or those with limited income. To ensure that all voices are heard, other options should be offered when possible, including paper surveys, phone calls, or information kiosks in community spaces.

Tools to consider include:

1. **Survey platforms:** Qualtrics, SurveyMonkey, Google Forms, KoboToolbox (for low-bandwidth settings)

2. **Mapping and visualization:** ESRI, Social Explorer, Tableau, PolicyMap

3. **CRM-integrated tools:** Salesforce Nonprofit Success Pack, Apricot by Bonterra

Ethical and Cultural Considerations in Data Collection

Every data collection strategy must prioritize informed consent, confidentiality, and cultural relevance. Questions should be translated into the preferred languages of the community and pre-tested for comprehension. Encouraging participation, through stipends, gift cards, or food, can increase response rates and show respect for participants' time.

Nonprofit leaders should also consider data sovereignty, especially when working with Indigenous, undocumented, or historically surveilled populations. Community members must understand how data will be used, stored, and shared, and should retain a voice in those decisions (Rainie et al., 2017).

Data collection is not simply about gathering information: it is a valuable pathway to build relationships and trust. The chosen methods and tools should reflect the values of inclusivity, transparency, and utility. When community members see themselves reflected in the data, and when the process honors their time and perspectives, the resulting assessment becomes both valid and meaningful.

Equity-Centered Practices

Conducting a needs assessment without a clear equity lens can reinforce the very disparities that nonprofit programs seek to address. Historically, data collection efforts have excluded marginalized voices, misrepresented communities of color, and used metrics that validate dominant cultural norms. Equity-centered practices aim to disrupt those patterns by embedding fairness, inclusion, and cultural humility in every stage of the assessment process.

Framing the Assessment with Equity in Mind

Before collecting data, nonprofit leaders must critically analyze the underlying assumptions driving the assessment. Who decides what counts as "need"? What narratives are emphasized in the framing of the inquiry? An equity-centered assessment explicitly recognizes power dynamics and makes space for those most affected by social inequities to help shape the process (Coulton et al., 2011).

This process begins by defining the meaning of equity in an organizational context and requires recognizing that equal treatment is not the same as equitable opportunity. Equity-based assessments examine root causes, structural barriers, and historical patterns of exclusion.

Disaggregating Data for Insight, Not Oversight

A review of overall data can convey the illusion of progress, but only an in-depth analysis of the numbers allows the real story to emerge. Data disaggregation by race, gender, language, age, geography, or disability status reveals patterns that might otherwise remain hidden to nonprofit leaders. For instance, while a city's average high school graduation rate may seem steady, a closer look might reveal that Indigenous youth or English language learners are graduating at significantly lower rates.

Applying this level of attention to detail is critical. It helps organizations to understand who is being left out and allows leaders to shape programs that respond to specific needs, while tracking progress toward equity goals over time; however, it must be done with care. Asking for demographic information requires sensitivity and clarity: people should know why the data is being collected and how it will be used, while always retaining the option to self-identify in ways that feel right to them - or to opt out entirely. When used carefully, disaggregated data becomes a tool for both understanding and resolving disparities.

Avoiding Deficit Framing

Too often, traditional assessments focus only on what communities don't have, such as jobs, quality schools, or safe housing—without recognizing the strengths and resilience that already exist. When we only look through this kind of "deficit lens," we risk reinforcing negative stereotypes and overlooking the ideas, talents, and aspirations of the very people we aim to support. A more balanced approach honors both the challenges and the assets present in communities. It invites communities to be seen, not just as recipients of help, but as partners in shaping solutions. Equity-centered approaches counter deficit framing by emphasizing community voice, recognizing strengths, and contextualizing challenges within systems, rather than focusing on individual failings (Dean-Coffey, 2018).

For example, if an assessment highlights low vaccination rates in a Black community, an equity lens would explore systemic mistrust rooted in medical racism, instead of simply labeling the community as resistant or uninformed.

Language Access and Cultural Relevance

Language justice is a cornerstone of equitable data collection. Surveys, interviews, and reports must be accessible in the community's languages, not only through translation and interpretation, but through culturally appropriate framing. Literal translation and interpretation alone do not ensure clarity or trust. Engaging bilingual staff or community translators and interpreters, and field-testing materials with local audiences, increases validity and inclusion.

Cultural relevance also extends to research design. Questions should reflect local realities and should avoid imposing frameworks that may be unfamiliar or irrelevant to participants. Indigenous evaluation methodologies, for instance, prioritize relational accountability, storytelling, and collective wisdom rather than individualized metrics (Chilisa, 2012).

Who Interprets the Data—and How

Equity-centered assessments go beyond simply gathering information from community members, it invites people to help make sense of the results. Instead of treating residents as research subjects, these approaches see them as co-interpreters and partners in the process. One powerful way to achieve this is using community validation sessions, where findings are shared with those who contributed to the assessment. These gatherings create space for feedback, clarification, and deeper conversation. They not only help to correct misinterpretations or fill in missing context but also build trust and ensure that the conclusions truly reflect the lived experiences of the people at the heart of the work.

Interpretation is not neutral. The lens through which data is analyzed influences conclusions and recommendations. Involving multiple perspectives, especially those of people directly affected, guards against bias and enhances credibility.

Equity is not a postscript - it must be present from the first framing of a needs assessment through to analysis and action. When nonprofit leaders approach assessment with cultural humility, an understanding of structural barriers, and a genuine willingness to share power, the results are not only accurate, but they are also fair and meaningful. This kind of equity-centered approach doesn't just check boxes: it helps to build programs that truly reflect the needs and strengths of the communities they are intended to serve. In the end, assessments rooted in equity lead to solutions that are more inclusive, more responsive, and more capable of creating lasting change.

Participatory Methods

Traditional needs assessments often treat community members as subjects to be studied. In contrast, participatory methods recognize members as co-creators of knowledge. These approaches emphasize the voices, insights, and leadership of people with lived experience, yielding more valid, relevant, and trusted data. Participatory assessment is more than a methodological choice, it is a practice rooted in equity, mutual respect, and shared power.

From Community Engagement to Co-Research

Participatory assessment involves more than consultation or outreach, transforming the role of community members from informants to collaborators. Residents help to shape research questions, choose data collection tools, interpret findings, and decide how information will be used. This approach democratizes knowledge production and honors community agency (Minkler & Wallerstein, 2008).

Core principles of participatory methods include:

1. Valuing lived experience as expertise.

2. Building relationships based on trust and reciprocity.

3. Redistributing decision-making power.

4. Investing time in mutual capacity building.

5. Tools and Approaches for Participation

Several tools and techniques support meaningful community participation in assessments:

1. **Community Advisory Boards (CABs):** Representative groups of residents who guide assessment design, data interpretation, and use of results.

2. **Photovoice:** A visual method where participants take photographs to represent their experiences and priorities, often paired with narrative reflection (Wang & Burris, 1997).

3. **Story Circles:** Facilitated discussions where participants share personal stories that illuminate systemic challenges or community assets.

4. **Mapping Workshops:** Residents map local resources, hazards, or opportunity zones using GIS or paper-based methods.

5. **Co-Design Labs:** Collaborative sessions in which stakeholders collectively identify problems and design interventions.

Each of these tools can be adapted to different populations and settings, with attention given to accessibility and cultural context.

Example: Photovoice in Action – Youth Homelessness

In 2023, a nonprofit serving homeless youth partnered with a local community college to conduct a Photovoice project aimed at deepening understanding of lived experiences. Rather than relying solely on survey data, the organization invited ten young participants ages 16 to 22 to document their daily lives using disposable cameras.

Over the course of three weeks, participants captured images that reflected both the challenges and resilience of their lives: sleeping in cars, sharing meals with peers, navigating resource centers, or finding beauty in abandoned urban spaces. Each photograph was accompanied by a short narrative or caption written by the participant.

Afterward, the nonprofit facilitated a gallery-style presentation of selected photos for staff, funders, and local policymakers. These visual narratives prompted powerful conversations about gaps in shelter access, safety concerns in existing services, and the need for youth-designed programming.

Impact:

1. The project led to the redesign of the organization's intake process, incorporating peer mentors and trauma-informed spaces.

2. A county foundation cited the exhibit in awarding a $75,000 grant for transitional housing tailored to LGBTQ+ youth.

3. Most importantly, participants reported increased confidence and a sense of agency—one youth later joined the nonprofit's advisory board.

"No one ever asked me what it feels like to live like this. This project made me feel seen."

—Photovoice participant

Compensation and Reciprocity

True participation requires recognizing the time, insight, and labor of community members. This recognition is expressed by offering stipends, covering transportation or childcare costs, and acknowledging contributions in reports or public presentations. Reciprocity is not just transactional but is a sign of respect and solidarity.

A failure to compensate participants runs the risk of perpetuating extractive practices, through which organizations benefit from community input without sharing resources, recognition, or outcomes.

Building Trust Through Process

Participatory methods often move more slowly than traditional assessments, requiring time to build relationships, co-develop processes, and navigate power dynamics. But the payoff is significant, manifesting itself in the form of higher quality data, increased community ownership, and stronger pathways to implementation.

When residents recognize their own voices reflected in the findings—and when they are part of the decision-making that follows—they are more likely to support, sustain, and advocate for resulting programs or policy changes.

Challenges and Commitments

Participatory assessment is not without its challenges. It demands humility from organizational leaders, flexibility in timelines, and a willingness to share control. Conflict or disagreement may arise, particularly when community priorities diverge from funder expectations or organizational agendas.

However, these tensions provide opportunities for learning and transformation. By making space for multiple truths, and by navigating discomfort with integrity, nonprofits model the type of inclusive, just processes that they hope to promote.

Participatory methods transform needs assessments into collective acts of reflection, inquiry, and design. These methods create more ethical, equitable, and effective assessments by fully engaging those most affected by the issues at hand. For nonprofit leaders committed to authenticity and impact, participatory assessment is not a luxury—it is a responsibility.

Data Analysis and Interpretation

Once data has been collected through surveys, interviews, focus groups, or participatory methods, the challenge becomes one of extracting meaning from the results. Data analysis and interpretation are not neutral acts—they reflect the assumptions, priorities, and frameworks of those conducting the assessment. To uphold ethical and equitable practice, nonprofit leaders must approach analysis as both a technical and relational process.

Moving from Raw Data to Insight

The goal of analysis is to synthesize information in ways that reveal patterns, clarify trends, and support informed decision-making. Quantitative data is often analyzed using descriptive statistics (e.g., frequencies, percentages, cross-tabulations), while qualitative data is coded for themes, narratives, and recurring concepts.

Key steps in the analytic process include:

1. Cleaning and organizing data for consistency and quality.

2. Grouping similar responses while identifying outliers.

3. Examining correlations or relationships among variables.

4. Comparing results against benchmarks, previous years, or peer communities.

Software tools such as Excel, SPSS, R (for quantitative data), or NVivo, Dedoose, and Atlas.ti (for qualitative data) can support rigorous analysis, but software or AI cannot replace reflective judgment or contextual understanding.

Engaging Multiple Perspectives

Inclusive interpretation improves validity and trustworthiness. Community validation sessions, in which preliminary findings are shared with participants for feedback, allow those closest to the data to verify its accuracy, offer context, or challenge assumptions.

For example, if survey data suggests low usage of a local clinic, community members might explain that the clinic's limited hours, cultural insensitivity, or lack of public transit access, rather than a lack of need, contributed to the results.

Including program staff, peer organizations, and community leaders in interpretation also fosters collaborative learning and ensures that conclusions reflect multiple realities.

Avoiding Common Pitfalls

Even the most thoughtfully designed needs assessments can fall short if the data is interpreted without care. One common misstep is overgeneralization - drawing sweeping conclusions from a sample that is too small or not representative of the broader community. While the data might be real, its reach is often overstated. Another risk is cherry-picking, through which only the findings that support a preferred narrative - often one that aligns with funder priorities or internal agendas - are highlighted. This not only distorts the picture, but also undermines trust in the process (Patton, 2015).

There is also a tendency in some assessments to ignore outliers— those responses that don't fit the dominant trend. Yet, these outlier perspectives frequently offer the most insight into systemic gaps or emerging needs (Preskill & Gopal, 2014). Likewise, the idea that data is somehow "neutral" can lead to false objectivity.

All data is collected and interpreted through human choices: what questions are asked, how these questions are framed, and whose voices are amplified. Ignoring these layers of bias can result in conclusions that appear superficially accurate, but miss deeper truths (Chilisa, 2012).

Avoiding these pitfalls takes more than technical skill. It requires humility, transparency, and a deep commitment to ethical practice. Analysts and nonprofit leaders must be willing to sit with complexity, challenge their own assumptions, and make room for voices that are often left out of dominant narratives. This form of honest, reflective analysis not only strengthens the credibility of the findings but also helps to ensure that the path forward is grounded in real community insight rather than what is easiest to measure or most comfortable to hear.

From Data to Actionable Findings

The final step in analysis is crafting a story that connects the data to real-world implications. Findings should be framed with clarity, contextualized with stakeholder voices, and organized around themes that relate to the organization's goals or theory of change.

Effective presentations of results often include:

1. Summary tables, infographics, or visual dashboards

2. Representative quotes or narratives to humanize statistics

3. Comparison points (e.g., peer regions, national benchmarks)

4. Clearly stated implications for programs, policy, or advocacy

Data analysis and interpretation are more than mere technical exercises—they are acts of leadership. When performed with care, collaboration, and equity in mind, analysis transforms raw information into meaningful insight. It closes the loop between inquiry and action, ensuring that community voices shape not only the data collected, but the story told and the strategy pursued.

From Assessment to Action

The transition from data collection to actionable planning begins with thoughtful synthesis. This step is far more than a summary; it is a strategic interpretation of the evidence gathered. A strong synthesis distills complex data into clear, cohesive insights that elevate both the challenges and strengths revealed during the assessment. It should highlight key themes, quantify major patterns, and reveal urgent or recurring concerns raised by the community. Just as importantly, it must emphasize local assets, existing initiatives, and community resilience, not just unmet needs. Framing the findings through both a strengths-based and needs-based lens ensures a more balanced and empowering narrative.

Effective summary reports make several critical distinctions. These reports differentiate between short-term issues that can be addressed through programmatic adjustments and longer-term structural needs that may require policy change or multi-year planning. Syntheses should also clarify which findings are immediately actionable within the organization's scope, and those which may warrant broader collaboration, such as forming new partnerships, advocating for policy reforms, or contributing to systems-level change.

By organizing information in this way, leaders help staff, board members, and community stakeholders to quickly grasp the assessment's core messages. Clear synthesis creates a shared foundation for decision-making, enabling teams to align strategies, prioritize initiatives, and allocate resources with confidence. In turn, this bridges the gap between research and practice, ensuring that data does not sit idle, but instead fuels progress rooted in community voices and evidence-based insight.

Communicating the Results

Sharing the results of a needs assessment is more than a final step, it is a key part of how trust is built and momentum is sustained. When findings are clearly and thoughtfully communicated, they do more than inform; they invite collaboration, validate community voices, and spark meaningful change. In many ways, the ways in which the results are shared matters as much as what the results say.

Effective communication requires meeting people where they are. Community members are more likely to engage with materials that are readily understood and culturally relevant, whether conveyed through a town hall, a translated summary sheet, or a visually engaging infographic. Funders, on the other hand, often look for structured reports that connect the dots between findings and the outcomes in which they have invested. Within the organization, staff may benefit from slide decks, dashboards, or guided sessions that help them to process the data and reflect on its significance in their day-to-day work.

Importantly, sharing results is more than a one-and-done event. It should be part of an ongoing conversation. Nonprofit leaders are doing more than reporting when they bring findings back to the community. Whether they are confirming interpretations, filling in missing context, or simply saying thank you, they are demonstrating that community input matters, and that participation is valued. This kind of reciprocity reinforces the collaborative spirit that makes assessments meaningful in the first place (Gupta, Fawcett, & Valdovinos, 2022).

Setting Priorities

Needs assessments inevitably uncover more issues than an organization can address at once, making strategic prioritization essential. Determining where to act first involves balancing several factors: the urgency of the need from the community's perspective, the organization's capacity to respond, the availability of resources, and alignment with mission and strategic goals.

To support thoughtful decision-making, many organizations use tools such as feasibility-versus-impact matrices to identify quick wins alongside high-value investments. Facilitated exercises such as stakeholder ratings or community listening sessions, help to introduce multiple voices to the prioritization process (Center for Community Health and Development, 2023). Equity audits can be particularly useful in ensuring that decisions serve to reduce, rather than reinforce, disparities (Keleher, 2020).

What matters most is that the process is grounded in clear, values-aligned criteria. When decisions are transparent and intentional, rather than reactive or politically motivated, organizations build internal clarity and external credibility.

Linking to Strategy and Program Design

Needs assessment findings should not sit on a shelf. They are most powerful when used to directly inform the organization's theory of change, strategic priorities, and program design. For example, if the data reveals a gap in mental health access among youth, the organization might respond by embedding behavioral health support in its existing programs. Geographic disparities in service access may suggest a need for mobile outreach or targeted site expansion. Identified community strengths, such as active neighborhood networks, could inspire new approaches to peer leadership or volunteer mobilization.

When programs are designed in response to lived experiences and documented needs, they are more likely to achieve meaningful impact and attract long-term support (Anderson, 2005; Community Tool Box, 2023).

Maintaining Accountability

Implementing change based on assessment findings is not the final step; rather it is part of an ongoing cycle of accountability. Transparency in this phase is critical. Communities and stakeholders need to see that results were not only collected, but that they mattered.

Organizations can build this accountability by publicly sharing progress updates, outlining what actions have been taken in response to the findings, and—equally important—explaining what has not been addressed and why. Creating spaces for ongoing community feedback ensures that the dialogue continues, and integrating impact evaluation plans allows organizations to revisit their original questions over time to assess what has changed (Preskill & Gopal, 2014).

When the community members can see a clear link between their input and tangible improvements, trust deepens. The organization's credibility grows, and future engagement becomes easier and more authentic.

The ultimate value of a needs assessment lies not in the volume of data collected, but in how that information is used. When findings are communicated with clarity, priorities are set with intention, and strategies evolve in response to real voices, the assessment becomes far more than a technical exercise. It becomes a vehicle for transformation. At its best, this process reflects a model of leadership that is curious, collaborative, and deeply committed to equity and accountability.

Case Study:
Participatory Assessment in Practice

To illustrate the principles outlined in this chapter, consider the following case study from a community-based organization operating in a rural region of the Pacific Northwest. The organization - let's call it Evergreen Horizons - serves a tri-county area with high poverty rates, limited public transportation, and a growing immigrant population.

Background and Purpose

Evergreen Horizons set out to redesign its family support programs after receiving feedback that existing services were not reaching the region's Spanish-speaking residents. The leadership team committed to conducting a participatory needs assessment to better understand barriers to access, community strengths, and service gaps.

Assessment Design

The assessment was designed in partnership with a bilingual Community Advisory Board (CAB) composed of parents, promotoras (community health workers), school staff, and youth leaders. The CAB helped to draft the research questions, reviewed tools for cultural appropriateness, and led community outreach.

Evergreen used a mixed-method approach:

1. **Quantitative data:** A bilingual household survey, distributed in paper and online formats, gathered information on service use, unmet needs, and demographic patterns.

2. **Qualitative data:** Promotoras facilitated story circles and one-on-one interviews in homes, churches, and mercados.

3. **Participatory tools:** Youth in the community used photovoice to document challenges and resources in their neighborhoods.

Data Collection and Interpretation

Over 300 surveys were completed, and 24 families participated in qualitative sessions. Key findings included:

1. High levels of social isolation among immigrant mothers

2.   Unmet needs for bilingual mental health support

3.   Concerns about discrimination at service access points

4.   Strong networks of informal caregiving and peer support

The CAB reconvened to interpret the data. Their discussions shaped the final recommendations and identified culturally specific strategies to reduce barriers.

From Findings to Action

The organization used the findings to:

1.   Launch a bilingual parent navigator program staffed by trusted community members

2.   Adjust service hours and locations based on transportation patterns

3.   Co-locate mental health screenings with ESL classes

4.   Secure new funding for mobile service delivery

The results were shared in a community celebration in which participants presented photo essays and led roundtable discussions with local policymakers.

Outcomes and Lessons Learned

A year after implementation, Evergreen Horizons reported increased service utilization among Spanish speaking families, improved client satisfaction, and stronger cross-sector collaboration. Just as importantly, community members reported feeling "seen and heard" in new ways.

This case demonstrates how participatory assessments can generate more than data—they can generate trust, leadership, and lasting change. By centering community voice throughout the process, Evergreen Horizons transformed its programs and its relationship with the people it serves.

Discussion Questions

1. What are the key differences among expressed, normative, felt, and comparative needs? Provide examples of how each might appear in a nonprofit setting.

2. How can equity-centered practices reshape the way we define and interpret community needs?

3. Describe at least three participatory tools used in needs assessments and discuss how they promote community voice.

4. What are the ethical considerations in collecting and analyzing community data?

5. Explain the value of disaggregated data in understanding equity gaps within a community.

6. Discuss the challenges and opportunities of translating needs assessment findings into strategic action.

7. How does involving community members in data interpretation improve assessment outcomes?

8. Reflect on the case study: What contributed to its success, and how might your organization replicate similar approaches?

Field Markers

1. **Asset-Based Community Development (ABCD):** A meth-

odology that focuses on identifying and leveraging existing strengths and resources within a community.

2. **Community Advisory Board (CAB):** A representative group of community members who guide and provide input on research, program design, or policy initiatives.

3. **Comparative Need:** A type of need identified by comparing access to services or outcomes across different populations or geographies.

4. **Data Disaggregation:** The process of breaking data into subcategories (e.g., by race, age, gender) to reveal disparities that might be hidden in aggregate data.

5. **Equity-Centered Assessment:** A strategy that actively considers and addresses systemic inequities in the design, implementation, and interpretation of needs assessments.

6. **Expressed Need:** A need that is clearly stated or demonstrated through action, such as high usage rates of a particular service.

7. **Felt Need:** A need based on individuals' perceptions or experiences, which may or may not be explicitly expressed.

8. **GIS (Geographic Information Systems):** Tools that map and analyze spatial data to uncover geographic patterns in community needs or assets.

9. **Logic Model:** A visual representation that links program resources, activities, outputs, and outcomes.

10. **Mixed-Method Assessment:** An evaluation strategy that combines quantitative and qualitative data collection and analysis.

11. **Normative Need:** A need identified by comparing a current state to a standard, benchmark, or expert recommendation.

12. **Participatory Methods:** Research or planning strategies

that engage community members as active participants, rather than passive subjects.

13. **Photovoice:** A participatory tool in which individuals use photographs to capture and discuss community conditions and concerns.

14. **Story Circle:** A method of gathering qualitative data by facilitating small group storytelling sessions around a common theme.

15. **Triangulation:** Using multiple data sources or methods to enhance the validity and reliability of assessment findings.

- Chapter 6 -

Measuring Program Outcomes

Nonprofit organizations operate in an increasingly data-driven environment, one in which accountability and transparency are essential to sustaining trust, securing funding, and demonstrating impact. Outcome measurement is no longer a supplementary task—it is central to ethical leadership and mission-aligned strategy. This chapter provides readers with a comprehensive framework for designing, implementing, and communicating evaluation practices that are both rigorous and equitable.

Learning Objectives

By the end of this chapter, readers will be able to:

1. Distinguish among outputs, outcomes, and impact.

2. Set measurable objectives aligned with mission and logic models.

3. Select appropriate tools and methods for different types of outcomes.

4. Use real-time monitoring and dashboards for adaptive management.

5. Understand and apply Social Return on Investment (SROI) frameworks.

6. Translate findings into continuous improvement strategies.

7. Communicate outcomes effectively and ethically to diverse stakeholders.

Quick-Glance Map

Section	Learning Objective
Outputs, Outcomes, and Impact	Differentiate among outputs, outcomes, and long-term impact.
Measurable Objectives	Formulate SMART goals linked to mission and logic models.
Tools and Methods	Choose appropriate qualitative and quantitative tools for various outcomes.
Dashboards and Monitoring	Implement real-time data tools for adaptive decision-making.
Longitudinal Evaluation	Track program effects and changes over extended timeframes.
Social Return on Investment (SROI)	Assess and express social value using financial proxies.
Continuous Improvement	Apply evaluation insights for iterative learning and program refinement.
Stakeholder Communication	Share outcomes transparently across diverse stakeholder groups.
Case Study	Analyze a real-world example of integrated evaluation practice.

Defining Outputs, Outcomes, and Impact

One of the most fundamental challenges in nonprofit evaluation is learning how to make the transition from describing activities to demonstrating change. While many organizations can readily list what they do, such as delivering workshops or providing meals, fewer can clearly articulate the differences those actions make in the participants' lives. In today's funding and policy environment, this distinction is more than technical; it is a matter of organizational credibility and ethical responsibility.

Outputs refer to the immediate, countable results of program activities. These are often required for compliance or reporting, such as the number of individuals served, workshops conducted, or items distributed. For example, a shelter might report that it distributed 400 hygiene kits, or that it served 120 youth through financial literacy classes. These numbers are important in demonstrating scale and reach, but they do not speak to transformation. If we stop here, we risk mistaking activity for impact (Hatry, 2006).

Outcomes, on the other hand, reflect the changes resulting from these activities. These could be shifts in behavior, knowledge, confidence, or conditions. Instead of only counting how many youths attended a class, we ask: Did their understanding of money management improve? Are they more confident in applying for jobs? Have they secured employment? Well-designed outcome measures help organizations move from "what we did" to "what changed because of what we did" (Kirkpatrick & Kirkpatrick, 2006).

Impact goes one step further, addressing the long-term, often systemic changes to which a program contributes. While more difficult to isolate and measure, impact tells the broader story, addressing such issues as whether communities experience lasting improvements in health, safety, education, or economic stability. For example, if job training programs contribute to lower unemployment rates across a region over several years, that would represent impact (Fitzpatrick, Sanders, & Worthen, 2011).

In practice, these distinctions are best illustrated through logic models. Consider a nonprofit that offers entrepreneurship training:

1. **Output:** 100 small business owners complete the training.

2. **Outcome:** 65% report improved business practices or reve-

nue gains within six months.

3. **Impact:** Over five years, the community sees higher employ-ment rates and reduced reliance on public assistance.

These levels of measurement are interdependent. Outputs create the conditions for outcomes, which, when scaled and sustained, may lead to impact. But overstating or confusing these terms can lead to unrealistic claims and a loss of trust. Ethical evaluation means acknowledging what we can measure, what we can reasonably claim, and how our work fits into a broader ecosystem of change (Ebrahim, 2019; Kania & Kramer, 2011).

Distinguishing among outputs, outcomes, and impact is not simply a technical exercise. It is a strategic and ethical imperative ensuring that nonprofit leaders remain accountable, tell truthful stories of change, and align their strategies with the communities that they serve.

Setting Measurable Objectives

Clear, measurable objectives are the foundation of any meaningful evaluation strategy. These objectives provide a bridge between a nonprofit's mission and the results that it hopes to achieve, translating broad aspirations into specific, actionable targets. Without well-defined objectives, organizations risk chasing activity without direction or results without relevance.

One of the most widely used frameworks for writing strong objectives is the SMART model. SMART stands for:

1. **Specific:** What exactly do you want to accomplish?

2. **Measurable:** How will you know when it has been achieved?

3. **Achievable:** Is it realistic given your resources and context?

4. Relevant: Does it align with your mission and your stake-holders' needs?

5. **Time-bound:** When will the objective be met?

Consider this objective:

Increase the percentage of youth who secure full-time employment within three months of program completion from 60% to 75% by December 2026.

This is a strong SMART objective because it:

1. Clearly defines the target population (youth completing the program).

2. Establishes a baseline (60%) and target (75%).

3. Sets a timeframe (by December 2026).

4. Focuses on an outcome, not just an activity.

However, SMART objectives are only part of the story. While they bring clarity and accountability, they may lead to overly narrow goals. For instance, a workforce program might meet its SMART goal of job placement, but fail to consider job quality, cultural fit, or long-term satisfaction. This is why objectives must be grounded in the broader frameworks of logic models or theories of change, which help to ensure that what is being measured truly reflects mission impact.

Aligning Objectives with Logic Models and Theories of Change

Measurable objectives work best when they are anchored in a

clear logic model or theory of change. These tools help to visualize the ways in which day-to-day activities connect to long-term goals, mapping out the steps from inputs and outputs to desired outcomes and impact.

For example, in a youth workforce development program, the theory of change might look like this:

1. **Inputs:** Staff, training curriculum, employer partnerships

2. **Activities:** Resume workshops, mentorship, job fairs

3. **Outputs:** Number of youth trained, resumes completed, employers engaged

4. **Outcomes:** Youth gain confidence and skills; secure jobs within 90 days

5. **Impact:** Long-term reduction in youth unemployment and increased economic mobility

When objectives are aligned with this framework, they provide a clear throughline that connects strategy to execution. This alignment also helps funders, board members, and staff to understand how each part of a program contributes to the big picture.

Common Pitfalls in Goal-Setting

Even with best intentions, many nonprofits fall into common traps when setting goals:

1. **Vagueness:** Objectives that are too broad or ambiguous, (e.g. "empower the community") fail to provide direction or measurable outcomes.

2. **Confusing activity with outcome:** Counting workshops or service hours is useful, but unless it is linked to a change in

knowledge, behavior, or condition, it misses the point.

3. **Over-promising:** Aspirational goals can be inspiring but may also lead to unrealistic expectations or mission drift if not grounded in capacity.

Underestimating equity considerations: Goals that ignore cultural context or systemic barriers can result in token outcomes or unintended harm.

For example, a literacy program might set a goal to have 90% of children reading at grade level within six months. But if that community faces housing instability, limited internet access, or language barriers, the goal may be misaligned with participants' lived realities.

Strong objectives are not just technically sound - they should be contextually aware, equity-informed, and revisited as conditions evolve. A good objective tells you not only what success looks like, but also whose success it measures, how it will be assessed, and whether it truly serves the mission.

To illustrate, let's return to the entrepreneurship program example:

Objective: "By June 2026, at least 70% of graduates will report increased monthly income through business operations, as measured by follow-up surveys at 3- and 6-month intervals." This objective not only meets SMART criteria but also is tied to the desired outcome of improved economic stability.

When crafting objectives, it is important to include the voices of those most affected by your work. Engaging community members, clients, or frontline staff in defining success can lead to more relevant, culturally informed, and equitable goals. Objectives that are co-created with stakeholders tend to be more meaningful, and are more likely to be achieved.

Finally, measurable objectives are not set in stone. As programs evolve, so should their goals. Regular review, data reflection, and willingness to revise objectives are hallmarks of strong, adaptive leadership. What matters most is not just whether goals are achieved, but whether these goals move your organization closer to the change it seeks to create.

Tools and Methods for Outcome Measurement

Once strong objectives are in place, nonprofit leaders must decide how to measure progress toward them. This step reflects ethics and inclusion as much as it does the data. The tools that we choose reflect what and who we value. Effective outcome measurement is not a one-size-fits-all exercise. It requires an intentional blend of rigor, relevance, and respect for the community being served.

Programs focused on skill-building or knowledge acquisition often begin with pre- and post-assessments. For instance, a digital literacy course might use quizzes before and after the training to determine how much participants have learned. These tools help quantify individual growth in a structured way.

Behavioral outcomes, such job retention or reduced substance use, often rely on administrative records or longitudinal follow-up. A youth employment program might track job placements through employer verification, then follow up at 6- and 12-month intervals to assess job stability. Meanwhile, emotional or attitudinal changes—such as increased self-confidence or sense of belonging—may be captured through surveys using validated scales or narrative reflection.

But numbers alone rarely tell the whole story. Qualitative tools, including interviews, story circles, or open-ended surveys, add essential texture. They can reveal the context that underlies outcomes and give participants a voice in how impact is understood. For example, a community health project might pair blood pressure data with interviews to explore how participants experience stress, support, and well-being in their daily lives.

Blending methods often yields the richest insights. A youth arts program might track attendance and school engagement (quantitative) while collecting student journals and reflections (qualitative). This combined approach provides a fuller picture of both participation and transformation.

It is also essential to ensure that tools are culturally appropriate and accessible. Language, literacy level, and technology access all influence participants' ability to engage in evaluation. A refugee resettlement agency, for example, may need to translate written materials, or provide interpreters, to conduct oral surveys that include non-English-speaking clients.

Digital tools have expanded the possibilities. Software like Salesforce Nonprofit Cloud, Apricot by Bonterra, and KoBo Toolbox helps nonprofits to gather, store, and analyze data efficiently. These platforms support real-time tracking and integrated reporting, offering insights that can guide timely decisions. However, technology must be paired with digital equity, ensuring that clients without smartphones, internet access, or comfort with online tools can still participate meaningfully.

Ethical considerations must also guide measurement choices. Asking deeply personal questions without adequate support, or using tools that reinforce deficit narratives, can do harm. Trauma-informed practices, consent protocols, and feedback loops should be embedded in all evaluation strategies.

Ultimately, selecting the right measurement tools requires that we ask: What are we trying to learn? Whom will this data serve? And how can we ensure that our evaluation honors the experiences of the people at its center? When designed with care, outcome measurement becomes more than a reporting requirement—it becomes a mirror that reflects how well we are living up to our mission.

Real-Time Monitoring and Data Dashboards

In a fast-paced, often unpredictable environment, nonprofit leaders need more than annual reports to guide decision-making—they need access to real-time insights. Real-time monitoring allows organizations to track progress, detect emerging issues early, and pivot strategies when necessary. One of the most effective tools for this is the data dashboard: a visual interface that displays key performance indicators (KPIs) in a form that is accessible, timely, and actionable.

Dashboard design reflects more than aesthetics, it reflects intention. Each metric displayed should exemplify elements truly valued by the organization. For example, a youth mentoring program might choose to track not only the number of mentor-mentee meetings, but also participant satisfaction, mentor retention, or school attendance. These indicators, when monitored regularly, can help staff assess the strength of relationships, identify engagement gaps, and adjust interventions as needed (Hale, 2018).

The technology behind dashboards has become increasingly accessible. Tools such as Tableau, Power BI, and Google Data Studio allow nonprofits to customize visual displays and automate data integration from spreadsheets, surveys, or CRM systems. Platforms like Apricot by Bonterra and Salesforce Nonprofit Cloud also offer built-in dashboard capabilities tailored to nonprofit workflows (Morariu, Athanasiades, & Gardner, 2013). These tools can centralize data across programs, track trends over time, and support collaborative learning.

Importantly, dashboards should not be designed for leadership alone. The most effective systems are used across teams, helping case managers to spot client needs, enabling program staff to identify areas of improvement or regression, and even engaging board members in understanding organizational performance. When staff can see and understand data in real time, they are more likely to make proactive, informed decisions.

Equity must also be central in the design and interpretation of dashboards. Disaggregating data by race, gender, language, geography, or disability status can reveal disparities that aggregate numbers conceal. For example, a housing program might show high average success rates, but when broken down by subgroup, it becomes clear that residents with limited English proficiency are being underserved. These insights can lead to program refinements, additional supports, or systemic advocacy.

Dashboards do have limitations. They often favor quantitative data, which can lead to an overemphasis on that which is easy to count, rather that which is most meaningful. They also require a strong data culture, in which staff are trained, encouraged to ask questions, and supported in interpreting what they see. Additionally, as with any technology, privacy and data ethics are paramount. Sensitive information should be protected through the use of clear permissions, anonymization, and secure platforms.

A compelling example comes from a community food bank that developed a real-time dashboard to track distribution trends across neighborhoods. By mapping this data against census demographics, organization members were able to identify gaps in service and shift delivery routes to reach isolated populations. The dashboard also enabled volunteers to understand where their work was making the greatest impact, reinforcing morale and commitment.

In short, real-time monitoring is about both speed and responsiveness. Dashboards translate raw data into insight, insight into action, and action into impact. When used thoughtfully, this tool empowers everyone in the organization to remain aligned, informed, and accountable.

Longitudinal Evaluation: Tracking Over Time

While dashboards provide a real-time snapshot of progress, many of the most important outcomes in nonprofit work unfold slowly, over months or even years. Longitudinal evaluation is the practice of tracking participants or community-level changes over extended periods to understand the durability and depth of program impact. This approach is especially valuable for initiatives that tackle complex social issues such as education disparities, chronic health conditions, or intergenerational poverty.

Imagine a youth workforce development program that reports high job placement rates three months after graduation. This short-term success is promising - but do those jobs last? Are participants advancing in their careers? Are their wages rising? Without long-term follow-up, it is difficult to answer these essential questions and refine the program accordingly.

Longitudinal evaluation can assume many forms. Some organizations follow the same group of participants over multiple time points (e.g., at intake, six months, one year, and two years). Others use external administrative data, including school records, employment databases, or public health registries, to assess outcomes across time. Mixed methods are often most effective, combining surveys or interviews with hard data to create a richer narrative of sustained change (Fitzpatrick, Sanders, & Worthen, 2011).

Maintaining contact with participants over time requires intentional planning. Attrition - when participants drop out of the evaluation - can skew results, especially if those who disengage differ systemically from those who remain. Nonprofits can reduce attrition through strategies like regular check-ins, personalized follow-up, flexible participation methods (e.g., phone, text, or in-person), and small incentives. Transparency is also key: participants should know how their data will be used, stored, and protected.

Technology has made longitudinal tracking more manageable. Many CRM systems now support timed follow-ups, automatic reminders, and integration with other data systems. For instance, a mentoring organization might use its CRM to send surveys every six months and track trends in mentees' school performance or employment outcomes. When used with appropriate safeguards, data-sharing agreements can also enable nonprofits to access long-term results without burdening participants.

Ethical considerations are heightened when engaging in long-term evaluation. It is essential to consider whose experiences are being tracked, how success is defined, and what narratives are being reinforced. Equity-focused evaluations must examine how race, class, disability, and other social factors shape long-term outcomes, and whether programs are closing or widening those gaps (Patton, 2015).

One instructive example comes from a transitional housing nonprofit that followed families for three years after program exit. Initial findings showed 80% stable housing at six months, but by the two-year mark, only 55% remained housed. This insight prompted the organization to add follow-up supports and peer mentorship. In the next cohort, two-year housing retention rose to 73%. Without longitudinal evaluation, this critical data and its constructive application would have been missed.

In summary, longitudinal evaluation assists nonprofit leaders in answering deeper questions: Did our impact last? Who experienced meaningful change? What factors helped or hindered long-term success? While it requires time, effort, and ethical care, the reward is a clearer understanding of how programs create enduring value in people's lives.

Social Return on Investment (SROI)

For nonprofit organizations operating in a climate of heightened accountability, Social Return on Investment (SROI) offers a powerful method to articulate the value of their work. SROI goes beyond traditional evaluation by assigning a financial proxy to the social, environmental, and economic outcomes that are created by a program. In doing so, it enables nonprofit leaders to tell a more comprehensive story that not only depicts change but demonstrates the value of that change.

Unlike financial return on investment (ROI), which focuses strictly on monetary profit, SROI attempts to quantify impact that might otherwise be intangible—such as improved mental health, stronger social networks, or reduced reliance on public systems. This method is particularly useful for organizations seeking to demonstrate value to funders, policy partners, or community stakeholders who wish to see the broader effects of their support (Nicholls, Lawlor, Neitzert, & Goodspeed, 2012).

An SROI analysis typically follows a structured process:

1. Identify key stakeholders.

2. Map outcomes using a theory of change.

3. Gather evidence and assign financial proxies to each outcome.

4. Estimate deadweight (what would have happened anyway) and adjust for attribution.

5. Calculate the ratio of social value created to investment made.

For example, a reentry support program might calculate that for every \$1 invested, \$4.25 in social value is generated through reduced recidivism, increased earnings, and lower emergency service use. This doesn't imply a literal cash return; rather, it is an estimate of the economic benefits accruing to individuals, families, and society.

In Chapter 3, we touched on how SROI can complement other fundraising and storytelling efforts. When paired with participant testimonials and outcome data, SROI can serve as a compelling advocacy tool. It resonates especially well with institutional funders and public agencies that require both qualitative and quantitative evidence of return.

Still, SROI is not without its challenges. Assigning financial value to human experiences such as increased hope, restored dignity, or cultural connection—is inherently imperfect. Practitioners often rely on public data or market analogs, which can vary in quality or relevance. Over-precision can also mislead: a calculated ratio might appear scientific while masking underlying assumptions.

To address this, best practices include:

1. Transparent documentation of methods and proxies.

2. Sensitivity testing to account for uncertainty.

3. Blending SROI with qualitative data and community voice.

Equity considerations are equally important. Programs serving historically marginalized communities may produce profound results that resist monetization. For instance, an arts program supporting Indigenous youth might transform identity, confidence, and cultural pride—yet struggle to express this impact in monetary terms. Nonprofit leaders should resist the urge to reduce these stories to ratios alone.

Instead, SROI should be viewed as one piece of a broader evaluation mosaic, one that is valuable in addressing certain audiences and questions, but most meaningful when interpreted alongside narrative evidence, participatory feedback, and mission alignment.

From Measurement to Continuous Improvement

Outcome data is only as valuable as the action it inspires. While evaluation often begins as a funder requirement or a compliance task, its greatest power lies in guiding learning and improvement. Nonprofits that embrace evaluation as an ongoing leadership function—rather than as a retrospective report—position themselves to adapt, grow, and deepen impact over time.

Continuous improvement is the practice of using evaluation findings to iteratively refine strategies, operations, and outcomes. This concept has appeared throughout the textbook—in Chapter 4, where we explored data-informed program design, and in Chapter 5, where we examined how community needs assessments evolve into responsive services. At its core, continuous improvement means creating space for reflection, asking hard questions, and being willing to adjust course when needed (Preskill & Torres, 1999).

One of the most effective ways to establish this mindset is to structure regular feedback loops. Program teams might hold quarterly data reviews to openly discuss both successes and shortfalls. For example, a mentoring organization might notice that participant satisfaction drops after three months. This insight could lead to changes in onboarding, mentor pairing, or additional check-ins, all based on real-time input.

Rather than wait for end-of-year evaluations, effective nonprofits make evaluation part of day-to-day management. Dashboards, outcome snapshots, and qualitative feedback tools allow staff to stay connected to program performance areas that need improvement. A youth services nonprofit might track attendance patterns, then use these patterns to adjust session timing or transportation support, improving accessibility in real time.

Data, however, is only helpful if it leads to action. Organizations must cultivate a culture where questions are encouraged, learning is safe, and failure is treated as a source of insight rather than blame. Leadership plays a critical role here. When executive directors and board members model curiosity and transparency, (asking, "What are we learning?" rather than "Did we succeed?") staff are more likely to bring forth honest reflections and bold ideas.

Equity is an essential lens for continuous improvement. If data reveals disparities in outcomes, (for example, lower completion rates among English learners or LGBTQ+ youth) those patterns must be examined with empathy and urgency. Improvement efforts should focus not only on technical fixes but also on structural barriers and inclusive practices (Patton, 2015).

One nonprofit health center developed a powerful model for continuous improvement. Each quarter, they convened cross-functional teams to review evaluation data, client feedback, and disaggregated outcome trends. These sessions led to tangible changes: revision of intake forms to be more trauma-informed, adjustment of service hours to better fit community needs, and a shift of resources to underperforming sites. Over time, both service quality and client trust improved.

Ultimately, measurement without reflection is static. But when nonprofits treat data as a dynamic leadership tool - asking what it reveals, how it affirms or challenges assumptions, and what can be done differently - these organizations become more responsive, equitable, and resilient. Continuous improvement is not about being perfect: its focus consists of being present, curious, and committed to doing better each day.

Communicating Outcomes to Stakeholders

Collecting outcome data is only part of the story. For that data to influence change, guide investment, and strengthen trust, it must be communicated effectively. Outcome communication involves more than reporting: it is a strategic and ethical act that builds transparency, fosters engagement, and reinforces a nonprofit's mission.

Different stakeholders need different kinds of information, delivered in different formats. Funders often seek concise, data-rich reports that demonstrate return on investment. Boards typically need insight into progress toward strategic goals. Program participants and community members, on the other hand, are more likely to value clear, culturally relevant stories that reflect their lived experiences and contributions.

As emphasized in Chapters 3, 4, and 5, stakeholder communication should be intentional, inclusive, and multi-directional. Publishing a static report is not enough. Instead, organizations should consider the ways in which outcome findings can inspire meaningful dialogue, invite feedback, clarify goals, and build shared ownership of results.

Formats should be adapted to the audience. Dashboards and

executive summaries might suit board members, while social media updates, translated infographics, or video testimonials may better engage community stakeholders. For example, a housing nonprofit could pair statistics about tenant stability with resident stories and visuals that illustrate improved living conditions. This blend of quantitative and qualitative data deepens understanding and helps people connect to emotionally and intellectually with the outcome data (Goodman, 2017).

Authenticity matters. Exaggerating impact, or understating challenges, can erode trust. Ethical communication demands acknowledgement of successes, as well as discussing areas in which improvement is needed and what the organization is doing in response. One education nonprofit published an annual impact brief that included both progress metrics and lessons learned. By openly sharing that their tutoring program had struggled with virtual attendance and what adjustments had been planned, they earned renewed support and valuable feedback from funders and parents alike.

Equity should also guide communication strategy. Data should be disaggregated to highlight disparities in outcomes, and communication should actively reach groups that may have been historically excluded. Language access, visual accessibility, and cultural relevance are not optional: these elements are essential to achieve true transparency.

Participatory communication methods can elevate stakeholder voice and increase the credibility of findings. Some nonprofits co-present evaluation results with program participants, or hold listening sessions in which findings are shared and interpreted in a group setting. These approaches shift the power dynamic of evaluation from something done "to" communities to something done "with" them (Guijt, 2014).

A compelling example comes from a youth development nonprofit that invited alumni to co-analyze survey data and co-author an outcome report. The final product included data tables, youth-created artwork, and quotes from participants, all organized around themes chosen by the group. This report resonated deeply with funders and community members, and it led to policy changes within the organization to strengthen alumni support.

Ultimately, outcome communication involves more than sharing results: it is a rich process that affirms core values. When organizations communicate with humility, clarity, and care, this fosters stronger relationships, deepens stakeholder trust, and ensures that impact not only measured, but is understood.

Case Study: From Metrics to Meaning

To bring the concepts of outcome measurement and continuous improvement to life, this section examines how one organization used data to report, reflect, adapt, and deepen its impact.

Case: Bridges to Opportunity (BTO)

Bridges to Opportunity is a regional nonprofit supporting young adults aged 16–24 through career development, counseling, and housing stabilization. Like many multiservice organizations, BTO faced the challenge of demonstrating long-term impact across diverse service areas. Internally, staff felt isolated; externally, funders sought more integrated outcomes and clearer reporting.

In response, BTO embarked on a strategic learning initiative grounded in the principles outlined in this chapter. They began by convening a participatory process to build a shared theory of change. Through cross-departmental workshops that included staff, community partners, and program alumni, the team identified key outcomes that cut across programs: stable employment, emotional well-being, and housing security.

After defining these outcomes, BTO developed a unified outcome dashboard. This tool tracked both quantitative and qualitative indicators, such as employment retention rates, mental health survey results, and participant reflections. The dashboard data was disaggregated by race, gender, geography, and program site, allowing the team to detect patterns and equity gaps.

Early findings revealed that, while overall job placement rates were high, rural youth and LGBTQ+ participants experienced significantly lower job retention. These insights spurred immediate action: BTO launched affinity-based peer mentorship groups, increased access to transportation stipends, and introduced trauma-informed supervisor training for employer partners. Within two quarters, job retention among these subgroups improved by 22%.

At the same time, BTO conducted a Social Return on Investment (SROI) analysis to better articulate its broader value. By quantifying reduced emergency housing use, increased tax contributions, and improved mental health outcomes, the organization estimated that every $1 invested returned $3.80 in social value. The SROI analysis, combined with youth testimonials and artwork, was compiled into a public impact report that increased donor engagement and led to a renewed multi-year grant from a major foundation (Nicholls et al., 2012).

Importantly, BTO didn't stop at data collection. Evaluation results were integrated into weekly staff huddles, quarterly board meetings, and community learning forums. Staff members began referring to "impact checkpoints" and celebrating outcome milestones. Youth participants were invited to co-present findings at town halls and in funder briefings, reinforcing shared ownership of success.

This case illustrates the fact that nonprofits, by treating evaluation as an inclusive, ongoing, and equity-centered process, move beyond compliance. They create a culture of learning in which outcomes are not simply tracked, but are used to build stronger programs, empower communities, and advance systems change.

Chapter Review and Discussion Questions

Outcome measurement is central to effective nonprofit leadership, offering a bridge between program intent and demonstrated results. This chapter provided a comprehensive examination of how nonprofit organizations can define, evaluate, and communicate their impact by implementing structured, equity-informed evaluation strategies. Beginning with clear distinctions among outputs, outcomes, and impact, readers learned how these elements function within a logic model to map the pathway from activity to social change.

Through the exploration of SMART objectives and their alignment with theories of change, the chapter emphasized the importance of setting goals that are specific, measurable, and contextually relevant. Tools and methods of outcome measurement were presented through a mixed-methods lens, encouraging the integration of both quantitative data and qualitative insights. Special attention was given to cultural competence and the ethical selection of tools, ensuring that evaluation practices do not marginalize or misrepresent the communities served.

Real-time dashboards and longitudinal evaluation approaches were highlighted as complementary strategies. Dashboards support rapid responsiveness, while long-term tracking enables organizations to assess the durability of their impact. Social Return on Investment (SROI) was introduced as a method for quantifying social value in financial terms, accompanied by a caution against the oversimplification of complex outcomes. The chapter also addressed how outcome data can be applied for continuous improvement, encouraging nonprofit leaders to foster learning cultures that use evaluation to strengthen, not punish, programs and staff.

Crucially, the chapter explored the communication of outcomes as a strategic and ethical responsibility, emphasizing that outcome findings should be communicated in a transparent, accessible, and audience-appropriate manner. Formats such as impact briefs, dashboards, infographics, and participatory sessions were presented as tools to engage diverse stakeholders. These practices help to ensure that data is not merely reported but interpreted in ways that support equity and shared understanding.

Finally, a case study demonstrated how one organization operationalized these tools and strategies. Through stakeholder engagement, disaggregated data analysis, real-time tracking, and SROI evaluation, the case illustrated the ways in which nonprofits can shift from activity-focused narratives to genuine accountability and community impact. Throughout the chapter, readers were reminded that meaningful measurement is not a technical exercise—it is a leadership imperative grounded in trust, learning, and equity.

Discussion Questions

1. How can nonprofit leaders balance quantitative rigor with narrative storytelling in communicating outcomes?

2. What are the risks of using outcome data punitively, and how can organizations instead promote a culture of learning?

3. Reflect on a program in your organization. How could it benefit from longitudinal evaluation? What would be needed to implement this evaluation?

4. In what ways can disaggregated data reveal equity challenges? How should organizations respond to these findings?

5. How can participatory approaches strengthen both the quality of evaluation and the relationships with stakeholders?

6. How would you explain the concept of SROI to a board member unfamiliar with evaluation terminology? What are its advantages and limitations?

7. Reflection Prompt Think of a time when your organization adjusted a program based on feedback or data. What led to that decision? How did it impact the program's effectiveness or stakeholder trust?

Field Markers

1. **Outputs:** The direct products or services resulting from program activities; typically measured in quantities (Hatry, 2006).

2. **Outcomes:** Short- to intermediate-term changes in knowledge, behavior, skills, or condition experienced by participants (Ebrahim & Rangan, 2014).

3. **Impact:** Long-term, systemic change that occurs at the societal or community level, often beyond a single organization's

control (Fitzpatrick, Sanders, & Worthen, 2011).

4. **SMART Objectives:** Goals that are Specific, Measurable, Achievable, Relevant, and Time-bound; a widely adopted goal-setting framework (Doran, 1981).

5. **Theory of Change:** A conceptual map linking activities to outcomes and impact, explaining how and why change is expected to happen (Knowlton & Phillips, 2012).

6. **Logic Model:** A visual representation of a program's resources, activities, outputs, outcomes, and impact (McLaughlin & Jordan, 2015).

7. **Real-Time Dashboard:** A dynamic visualization tool displaying live performance data for decision-making (Morariu, Athanasiades, & Gardner, 2013).

8. **Longitudinal Evaluation:** The process of measuring outcomes over extended time periods to assess durability and delayed effects (Patton, 2015).

9. **Social Return on Investment (SROI):** A framework that estimates the social, environmental, and economic value created per dollar invested (Nicholls et al., 2012).

10. **Continuous Improvement:** An organizational commitment to using evaluation findings to iteratively refine strategies and practices (Preskill & Torres, 1999).

Chapter 7

Leadership and Change Management

Why Leadership and Change Management Matter

Change is not an occasional event in nonprofit leadership. It is a constant undercurrent. Whether a nonprofit leader is responding to shifts in funding, new policy mandates, community needs, or internal transitions, they must be skilled in managing uncertainty and guiding their organizations through disruption. Change management, when done well, is not only about planning and implementation. It is about communication, empathy, trust-building, and mission fidelity.

Effective change leadership is not just about mastering management tools or following a checklist, it's about people. At its core, leading change is a relational endeavor. It begins with a compelling vision, but it is brought to life through the leader's ability to engage others, build trust, and cultivate shared purpose.

Change rarely unfolds in a linear or predictable way. Instead, it often emerges in messy, uncertain, or resistant environments. In these moments, it's not enough to have a plan; leaders must navigate discomfort with empathy, communicate with clarity, and model resilience. When progress stalls or resistance arises, as it inevitably will, effective leaders do not abandon the vision. Rather, they adapt their strategies, listen deeply, and respond transparently, all while remaining anchored in purpose.

This capacity to lead with both courage and compassion distinguishes technical managers from transformational leaders. In the nonprofit sector, where missions are deeply personal, and change often intersects with community trauma or systemic injustice, this human-centered approach is not optional. It is the foundation of meaningful and sustainable change.

This balance of inspiration, collaboration, and grit is what separates technical managers from transformational leaders. As this chapter explores, managing change is not an abstract theory but a practical leadership skill that determines whether an organization can survive and thrive amid volatility.

This chapter offers a grounded, strategic, and human-centered approach to change. It begins with the leading theories and models used to frame organizational transitions. From there, it turns to applied leadership practices, such as navigating resistance and fostering psychological safety. The final sections explore the connection between change and leadership legacy, including succession planning and the importance of building organizations that are resilient beyond any single individual.

As you move through this material, consider the changes your organization has experienced over the past three years. What worked? What could have gone differently? The insights in this chapter are not only theoretical. They are meant to equip you with the skills to shape your organization's next chapter with clarity and confidence.

Learning Objectives

By the end of Chapter 7, readers will be able to:

1. Describe foundational theories and models of organizational change.

2. Analyze the role of leadership in navigating uncertainty and building resilience.

3. Apply principles of change management to real-world non-

profit scenarios.

4. Evaluate strategies for responding to resistance, fostering inclusion, and ensuring psychological safety.

5. Formulate approaches to succession planning that sustain leadership capacity beyond individual tenure.

Quick-Glance Map of Chapter 7

Section	Learning Objective
Theories and Models of Change Management	Compare and apply major change management models.
Leading Through Transitions and Challenges	Identify leadership strategies for managing internal and external disruption.
Navigating Resistance and Cultivating Buy-In	Analyze methods for reducing resistance and building stakeholder trust.
Adaptive vs. Transformational Leadership	Differentiate between adaptive and transformational approaches to leadership.
Creating Psychological Safety During Change	Demonstrate how to foster psychological safety during organizational change.
Succession Planning and Leadership Sustainability	Design sustainable succession strategies to support long-term organizational health.

Theories and Models of Change Management

Effective change leadership is ultimately a human endeavor. While technical tools and structured plans have their place, they are not what inspires people to move forward through uncertainty. Real change begins with a vision, something people can see themselves in, but it takes more than vision to get there. It takes trust, empathy, and the ability to meet people where they are. In the face of doubt, delays, or resistance, strong leaders don't retreat. They listen. They recalibrate. They keep the mission front and center while adjusting the path as needed. What defines transformational leadership isn't perfection or control, it's the capacity to stay grounded in purpose, invite others into the process, and persist with integrity even when the outcome is not yet in sight. How that change is introduced, managed, and sustained determines whether an organization evolves or fragments. For this reason, nonprofit leaders must not only understand the theory behind change but also know how to translate it into practice.

One of the earliest and most enduring models of organizational change is Kurt Lewin's three-stage framework. Developed in the 1940s, it views change as a dynamic process with three phases: unfreeze, change, and refreeze. The unfreezing stage involves preparing the organization for change by surfacing dissatisfaction with the status quo. The change phase centers on introducing new behaviors, systems, or structures. Finally, the refreezing stage is about solidifying new practices, so they become normalized and sustainable.

An example comes from a small rural education nonprofit that had relied for decades on paper-based volunteer intake forms. When new grant requirements demanded digitized records, the organization applied Lewin's model: first by unfreezing existing habits through discussion of inefficiencies and compliance risks, then by introducing a simple online form during staff training, and finally by celebrating the new process in team meetings and embedding it into onboarding materials. Though seemingly small, this shift significantly improved data integrity and reporting speed.

Recognizing the limitations of Lewin's model in large-scale or continuous change environments, John Kotter developed an eight-step process that emphasizes momentum and cultural embedding. These steps include creating urgency, building a guiding coalition, developing and communicating a strategic vision, enabling action, generating short-term wins, and anchoring the change into organizational culture (Kotter, 2012).

One example comes from a regional youth services nonprofit that faced declining program enrollment and waning donor interest. Leadership used Kotter's model to create urgency around long-term sustainability. A cross-functional task force of board members and frontline staff developed a new service model centered on family engagement. By piloting a small, high-visibility program and celebrating early successes publicly, the organization built internal enthusiasm and increased funder interest. Over time, staff began to view innovation as integral to the organization's identity.

For organizations undergoing individual-level changes such as adopting a new data system or reassigning program staff, Jeff Hiatt's ADKAR model offers an efficient, people-centered approach. ADKAR stands for Awareness, Desire, Knowledge, Ability, and Reinforcement. It outlines the sequence of outcomes individuals must achieve to embrace and maintain a change (Hiatt, 2006).

A housing nonprofit that transitioned from handwritten maintenance logs to a mobile app used the ADKAR model to guide staff adaptation. First, leadership explained the reasons for the change (Awareness) and held listening sessions to understand staff concerns (Desire). Then, they hosted hands-on tutorials (Knowledge), provided one-on-one coaching in the field (Ability), and gave recognition in staff newsletters for successful adopters (Reinforcement). This intentional rollout helped reduce resistance and increased staff confidence in the new system.

While each of the models described so far emphasizes either structure or personal transition, Appreciative Inquiry (AI) offers a more organic, strength-based model rooted in what is already working.

Developed by David Cooperrider and colleagues, AI moves through four phases: Discover, Dream, Design, and Deliver (Cooperrider & Whitney, 2005). Instead of starting with problems, AI invites organizations to amplify success.

Consider a community foundation undergoing a leadership transition. Rather than viewing the change as a disruption, the interim director used Appreciative Inquiry to facilitate conversations about what staff and community partners most valued about the organization. They co-created a vision for a more collaborative leadership structure, piloted team-led initiatives, and integrated these learnings into the recruitment and onboarding of the next executive director. The process preserved morale and deepened staff engagement during a potentially destabilizing period.

Ultimately, selecting the right model depends on the nature of the change, the organization's culture, and the level of stakeholder engagement required. What matters most is not adherence to a specific framework but the ability to lead with clarity, consistency, and compassion. Leaders who understand these models (and can bring them to life with practical examples) are better positioned to choose the right tools at the right time and to adapt as needed when the path forward shifts.

Choosing the Right Change Management Model: A Practical Guide

The following questions can help leaders assess which framework is most appropriate for their change initiative. While no model is a perfect fit, this tool can support intentional alignment between context, stakeholders, and strategy.

Consideration	If yes, consider...
Is the change relatively small in scope and requires step-by-step structure?	Lewin's Three-Stage Model
Is the organization facing an urgent challenge that requires broad cultural buy-in?	Kotter's Eight-Step Model
Is individual adoption the key to success (e.g., new technology or policy)?	ADKAR Model
Is the challenge ambiguous or rooted in values conflict with no clear solution?	Appreciative Inquiry (AI)
Is the organization experiencing a leadership transition or seeking renewal through staff engagement?	Adaptive Leadership
Is the change anchored in mission expansion, requiring deep vision and staff inspiration?	Transformational Leadership

Reflection Tip: Consider layering models when appropriate. For example, AI can be used in the early stages of a Kotter-based process, or ADKAR principles can support the implementation phase of an adaptive effort. What matters most is not adherence to a specific framework but the ability to lead with clarity, consistency, and compassion. Leaders who understand these models and can bring them to life with practical examples are better positioned to choose the right tools at the right time and to adapt as needed when the path forward shifts.

Leading Through Transitions and Challenges

While models and frameworks provide valuable scaffolding for understanding organizational change, the lived experience of guiding a team through transition is far more complex. Transitions are emotional, not just operational. They often involve uncertainty, loss, and redefinition of roles or identity. For nonprofit leaders, the challenge lies not only in managing logistical shifts but also in holding space for the human dynamics that accompany them.

The literature on change leadership consistently affirms that most initiatives fail not because the plan was flawed, but because the transition was mismanaged (Kotter, 2012). When stakeholders feel confused, ignored, or unsupported, even the most technically sound strategy can falter. Therefore, one of the most critical responsibilities of a nonprofit leader during change is to serve as a translator between strategy and staff experience.

Transitions vary in scope and intensity. Some involve incremental shifts, such as adopting a new data platform or revising a reporting protocol. Others may involve deeper realignment, like merging with another organization or redefining the program model. In all cases, leaders must anticipate emotional responses ranging from excitement and relief to fear and grief and create space for these to be acknowledged and addressed.

Research on organizational behavior underscores the importance of clear, consistent, and compassionate communication during transitions. According to Bridges (2009), successful change efforts distinguish between change (the external event) and transition (the internal process people go through). Leaders who recognize this distinction can better support their teams by explaining not just what is changing, but why it matters and how it will unfold.

Equally important is modeling calm and confidence. Leaders set the emotional tone of an organization. During times of flux, staff and stakeholders look to leadership for cues on how to interpret uncertainty. This does not mean feigning certainty or perfection. It means being transparent about what is known and unknown and demonstrating a steady commitment to organizational values throughout the process.

One often overlooked strategy is the use of "transition rituals." These are symbolic acts that help teams process change and mark new beginnings. Examples include launching a new initiative with a staff gathering, honoring a departing leader with stories of impact, or holding reflection sessions after a major restructuring. While they may seem peripheral, these rituals play a crucial role in restoring meaning and connection during organizational shifts (Heifetz et al., 2009).

Leaders should also pay attention to timing and pacing. Abrupt transitions, especially those perceived as top-down, can undermine trust. Conversely, overly drawn-out processes can create fatigue and confusion. Effective leaders strike a balance, sequencing change in manageable phases and maintaining momentum without overwhelming their teams. The use of feedback loops, including pulse surveys, staff listening sessions, and anonymous Q&A channels, ensures that leadership remains responsive throughout the transition period.

Finally, transitions should be framed not only as a response to external pressures, but as opportunities for organizational learning and renewal. When staff are invited into the change process as co-creators rather than passive recipients, they are more likely to invest in outcomes. Leaders who foster a culture of reflection, experimentation, and shared ownership position their organizations not merely to survive change, but to grow from it.

Navigating Resistance and Cultivating Buy-In

Every change initiative, no matter how well-intentioned or strategically sound, will encounter resistance. In the nonprofit context, this resistance is rarely about stubbornness. More often, it reflects a fear of losing identity, a perceived threat to mission integrity, or a concern that stakeholder voices are being overlooked. Nonprofit leaders must anticipate resistance not as a roadblock, but as a signal: it reveals where clarity is needed, where trust must be rebuilt, or where inclusion has been insufficient.

Understanding the origins of resistance is critical. It may stem from uncertainty about new expectations, lack of confidence in leadership, or concern about resource allocation. In mission-driven organizations, resistance is also frequently values-based. Staff and volunteers who joined because of shared ideals may fear that change could compromise those commitments. Leaders must listen deeply to these concerns, not to immediately counter them, but to understand the emotions and principles beneath the pushback.

Research shows that inclusive processes are one of the most effective antidotes to resistance. When people are invited to change planning early and meaningfully, they are more likely to support implementation (Lines, 2004). This does not mean every stakeholder must agree on every detail. It means that they should feel heard, respected, and informed. Transparent communication, particularly in the early stages, is essential. Leaders should clearly articulate the rationale for change, the expected impact, and the mechanisms for feedback and adaptation along the way.

One effective strategy for building buy-in is identifying and empowering internal champions, staff, board members, or volunteers who believe in the change and can model engagement to their peers. These champions are especially important in peer-to-peer communication, where trust is often strongest. Their involvement can also serve as an early indicator of which messaging strategies are resonating and which need recalibration.

It is also important to separate legitimate resistance from misinformation or fear-based narratives. Leaders must strike a balance between validating concerns and correcting false assumptions. This requires more than memos. It requires dialogue. Town halls, listening sessions, and one-on-one conversations provide space for mutual understanding. Leaders who engage in these practices demonstrate a willingness to be in relationship, not just in control.

Another helpful approach is to anticipate resistance points in advance. Scenario planning tools, commonly used in strategic planning, can be adapted to change processes by mapping potential sources of resistance and brainstorming preemptive responses. For example, when rolling out a new performance evaluation system, a leadership team might anticipate concerns about fairness, data privacy, or workload. By proactively addressing these in training materials or FAQs, the rollout feels less abrupt and more responsive.

Finally, leaders must avoid viewing resistance as a hurdle to be overcome quickly. When engaged thoughtfully, resistance can become a powerful contributor to adaptive change. It pushes leaders to clarify intentions, revisit assumptions, and sometimes slow down to ensure alignment. Those who once resisted can become some of the strongest advocates if they are engaged with humility and care.

Resistance is not the opposite of buy-in. It is the pathway to it. By treating resistance as a form of communication, rather than defiance, nonprofit leaders can transform challenge into collaboration and skepticism into shared purpose.

Adaptive vs. Transformational Leadership

Leadership during times of change is not a one-size-fits-all endeavor. The approach a leader takes must match the scale, urgency, and context of the challenge at hand. Two leadership approaches, adaptive and transformational, are particularly relevant in the nonprofit sector, where rapid shifts in funding, policy, and community needs demand both flexibility and vision.

Adaptive leadership, a framework introduced by Heifetz and colleagues (2009), emphasizes the capacity to navigate complex, uncertain situations where technical solutions do not yet exist. Adaptive leaders do not simply apply known answers to familiar problems. Instead, they diagnose emerging challenges, distribute responsibility, and engage stakeholders in experimentation and learning. In practice, this might look like facilitating cross-functional teams to co-design a new service delivery model or holding structured dialogue sessions to unpack racial equity concerns raised by frontline staff.

The hallmark of adaptive leadership is not control, but curiosity. Leaders must be willing to acknowledge discomfort, suspend immediate judgment, and resist the urge to resolve tension prematurely. Adaptive work often involves "getting on the balcony" - a metaphor for stepping back to gain perspective on the patterns, values, and loyalties that shape organizational responses to change (Heifetz et al., 2009). From this vantage point, leaders can more effectively challenge assumptions, recognize competing narratives, and surface underlying conflicts.

Transformational leadership, on the other hand, is rooted in the ability to inspire, motivate, and align people around a shared vision. First articulated by Burns (1978) and later expanded by Bass and Avolio (1994), transformational leadership seeks to elevate both individuals and the organization. Leaders in this model build trust through integrity and empathy, stimulate innovation by questioning the status quo, and support personal development by mentoring others. In non-profit settings, transformational leaders often emerge during periods of renewal, such as launching a strategic plan or founding a new social enterprise.

Both adaptive and transformational leadership are critical to managing change effectively, but they serve different functions. Adaptive leadership is best suited to ambiguous, high-stakes situations where solutions are not readily available. Transformational leadership is most potent when clear goals exist but require a cultural shift, increased motivation, or deep engagement to achieve. A leader responding to an external audit may need adaptive skills to rethink internal processes in real time. That same leader, championing a shift toward trauma-informed care, will need transformational capacities to shift the mindset and practice across the organization.

Effective nonprofit leaders blend these approaches. They know when to probe and when to galvanize, when to hold space for uncertainty and when to declare direction. They also recognize that leadership is not about personal charisma but about cultivating conditions in which others can act with courage and clarity.

In an increasingly volatile environment, the ability to flex between adaptive and transformational roles is no longer optional. It is the essence of resilient, responsive, and values-aligned leadership.

Creating Psychological Safety During Change

Change initiatives often falter not because they lack technical precision, but because they fail to consider the emotional and relational landscape of the organization. When staff feel unsafe emotionally, professionally, or psychologically, they are less likely to take risks, ask questions, or have surface concerns. For nonprofit leaders navigating periods of disruption, fostering psychological safety is not a luxury. It is a prerequisite for effective change.

Psychological safety, as defined by Edmondson (1999), refers to a shared belief that it is safe to take interpersonal risks within a team. This includes admitting mistakes, challenging ideas, expressing vulnerability, or acknowledging uncertainty. In the context of change management, psychological safety enables staff to engage with change openly rather than defensively. It transforms resistance into inquiry and compliance into commitment.

Leaders can foster this environment in several ways. First, they must model transparency. When leaders acknowledge what they do not know, admit past mistakes, and share the rationale behind difficult decisions, they demonstrate that imperfection is not a disqualifier for leadership; it is a hallmark of integrity. This type of leadership presence signals to staff that authenticity is not only permitted but valued.

Second, leaders must respond constructively to feedback. When employees voice concerns, ask challenging questions, or raise dissenting views, the response they receive matters deeply. Punitive or dismissive reactions create a chilling effect. In contrast, curiosity and gratitude build trust. Leaders who thank staff for speaking up, even when it is uncomfortable, cultivate a climate where learning is continuous and mistakes are seen as part of growth.

The physical and social environment also matters. Staff must have designated spaces where dialogue can occur without fear of retribution. This may include anonymous feedback tools, confidential coaching opportunities, or protected spaces in team meetings for open dialogue. Regular check-ins and inclusive facilitation techniques, such as using open-ended questions and rotating speaking roles, ensure that all voices are heard, not just the most senior or extroverted.

Importantly, psychological safety is not a license for complacency. It does not mean avoiding accountability or lowering standards. Edmondson (2019) emphasizes that the most effective teams are those that pair high psychological safety with high performance expectations. For nonprofit leaders, this means clearly communicating desired outcomes while remaining responsive to how people experience the path to those outcomes.

One case example involves a community health nonprofit that undertook a major restructuring after losing a key federal grant. Rather than framing the cuts as purely budgetary, the leadership team engaged staff in facilitated conversations about priorities, trade-offs, and lessons from previous change efforts. They encouraged anonymous feedback through weekly digital surveys and publicly reported themes that emerged. Staff who initially feared layoffs later cited the process as one of the most trust-building moments in the organization's history.

Creating psychological safety requires time, intention, and consistency. It is less about launching new programs and more about shifting how power is held, how dialogue is facilitated, and how learning is integrated into the culture. In periods of change when uncertainty is high and emotions run deep, this kind of leadership becomes not only protective, but transformative.

Succession Planning and Leadership Sustainability

In the nonprofit sector, where leadership transitions often occur with little warning and limited preparation, succession planning is both a strategic necessity and a moral imperative. Unlike corporations that may have formal talent pipelines and HR departments dedicated to leadership development, many nonprofits operate with lean infrastructure and reactive personnel strategies. As a result, the departure of a founder, executive director, or key program manager can cause significant disruption to mission continuity, stakeholder trust, and team morale.

Succession planning is not about naming a replacement. It is about building the conditions for leadership to thrive beyond any one individual. It is about ensuring that institutional knowledge, core values, and critical relationships are preserved and carried forward. In this way, succession planning is not merely risk mitigation; it is an investment in organizational resilience.

At its core, succession planning requires nonprofit leaders and boards to engage in honest dialogue about roles, vulnerabilities, and the future. This includes identifying mission-critical positions, assessing the organization's bench strength, and creating opportunities for leadership development across all levels. Formal tools such as talent matrices, cross-training plans, and mentoring programs can help institutionalize this process. Still, they are only effective when embedded within a culture that values learning and transparency.

One of the most common mistakes in succession planning is treating it as a confidential process. While board discussions around executive succession must respect confidentiality and personnel boundaries, the broader organization benefits from a transparent and participatory approach to leadership development. When staff see succession as a normal part of organizational life rather than a taboo topic, it becomes easier to cultivate future leaders and normalize change.

Succession planning also involves attending to the emotional and relational dimensions of transition. Leaders who are preparing to step down, particularly founders or long-tenured executives, often carry deep personal identification with the organization. Boards must support them through this transition while ensuring that the process centers on organizational needs. Similarly, incoming leaders should be given onboarding support and access to historical context so they can lead with both fresh perspective and institutional continuity.

For organizations without a formal succession plan in place, a good starting point is to conduct a leadership sustainability assessment. This involves asking questions such as:

1. Which roles are most critical to organizational functioning?

2. What knowledge would be lost if specific individuals departed tomorrow?

3. What processes exist for leadership development and knowledge transfer?

4. How do we prepare for both planned and unplanned transitions?

In times of crisis or rapid change, succession planning may feel like a distant priority. But it is precisely in these moments that the absence of a plan is most felt. Proactive organizations use stable periods to build the leadership infrastructure that will carry them through future disruptions.

Succession is not the end of leadership. It is its continuation. By approaching leadership transitions with foresight, humility, and shared responsibility, nonprofit leaders ensure that their organizations remain anchored in mission, equipped for change, and positioned for lasting impact.

Discussion Questions

1. Reflect on a time when your organization experienced significant change. What leadership approaches were used, and how effective were they?

2. How can nonprofit leaders distinguish between technical problems and adaptive challenges when responding to disruption?

3. In your organization, what signs would indicate that psychological safety is either present or lacking?

4. What practical steps could you take to begin developing a succession plan, even if leadership transitions are not immediately expected?

5. Which of the change management models presented in this chapter most closely aligns with your organizational culture? Why?

Field Markers

1. **Change Management:** A structured approach to transitioning individuals, teams, or organizations from a current state to a desired future state.

2. **Lewin's Three-Stage Model:** A foundational model that conceptualizes organizational change in three phases: unfreezing, changing, and refreezing.

3. **Kotter's Eight-Step Model:** A sequential framework for managing organizational change by establishing urgency, building coalitions, and embedding change into culture.

4. **ADKAR Model:** A change model focused on individual transitions, standing for Awareness, Desire, Knowledge, Ability, and Reinforcement.

5. **Appreciative Inquiry (AI):** A strengths-based approach to organizational change emphasizing inquiry, visioning, and collaborative design.

6. **Adaptive Leadership:** A leadership approach that emphasizes flexibility, learning, and shared problem-solving in response to complex challenges.

7. **Transformational Leadership:** A leadership style focused on inspiring and motivating teams to achieve change through vision, integrity, and development.

8. **Psychological Safety:** A team climate characterized by interpersonal trust and mutual respect, where people feel safe to take risks and be vulnerable.

9. **Succession Planning:** A strategic process for preparing and supporting transitions in key leadership positions to ensure continuity and resilience.

Chapter 8

Strategic Partnerships and Cross-Sector Collaboration

Building Relationships That Amplify Mission Impact

In an increasingly interconnected world, no nonprofit organization can afford to operate in isolation. Addressing complex social issues such as homelessness, food insecurity, racial inequity, or environmental justice requires coordination among nonprofits, government agencies, private sector actors, and community leaders. Strategic partnerships and cross-sector collaboration have become essential tools for advancing mission outcomes, expanding reach, and sustaining impact (Bryson et al., 2015).

This chapter explores how nonprofit leaders can cultivate effective partnerships that go beyond transactional cooperation. It examines the core principles of collaborative leadership, offers practical strategies for stakeholder alignment, and highlights common pitfalls in partnership formation and governance. From shared measurement systems to joint ventures, strategic collaboration can take many forms. The challenge for leaders is to design and steward these efforts in a way that is values-aligned, equitable, and results-oriented (FSG, 2014; Kania & Kramer, 2011).

We will begin by defining what strategic partnerships are and what they are not. We'll then delve into models of collaboration, including collective impact frameworks and public-private alliances. Later sections focus on building trust across institutional and cultural boundaries, negotiating shared decision-making, and managing power dynamics in multistakeholder settings. The chapter concludes with tools for evaluating collaborative effectiveness and sustaining partnerships over time (Emerson et al., 2012).

As you engage with this material, consider the ecosystems in which your organization operates. Who are your natural allies? Where is duplication occurring? What would it take to move from coordination to true collaboration? The future of nonprofit leadership rests in our ability to work better, together.

Learning Objectives

By the end of this chapter, readers will be able to:

1. Define strategic partnerships and differentiate them from informal coordination or competition.

2. Identify and evaluate models of cross-sector collaboration relevant to nonprofit contexts.

3. Apply principles of collaborative leadership to build and sustain mission-aligned partnerships.

4. Recognize common challenges in partnership governance, decision-making, and accountability.

5. Assess the effectiveness and equity of existing partnerships using practical evaluation tools.

Quick-Glance Map of Chapter 8

Section	Learning Objective
Defining Strategic Partnerships and Collaboration	Distinguish partnership types and clarify nonprofit roles and motivations
Models of Collaborative Engagement	Analyze collective impact, backbone organizations, and other structural models

Building and Sustaining Trust-Based Partnerships	Apply trust-building strategies and cultural fluency to collaborative settings
Governance, Power, and Shared Decision-Making	Examine governance structures and power dynamics in multi-stakeholder work
Evaluating Collaborative Success	Develop criteria and tools for assessing the impact and equity of partnerships

Defining Strategic Partnerships and Collaboration

Strategic partnerships are more than cooperative relationships; they are mission-driven alliances grounded in mutual benefit, shared risk, and collective impact (Kania & Kramer, 2011). In the nonprofit sector, such partnerships can extend across organizational boundaries and sectoral divides, encompassing collaborations with other nonprofits, government agencies, academic institutions, funders, or private companies. These arrangements are often formalized through memoranda of understanding (MOUs), joint funding proposals, or collaborative governance structures, but the heart of partnership lies in shared purpose (Bryson et al., 2015).

Not all partnerships are strategic. Coordination, for example, involves basic information-sharing to avoid duplication. Collaboration, by contrast, requires joint planning, pooled resources, and shared accountability. Competition, at the opposite end of the spectrum, occurs when organizations vie for the same funding or clients. Strategic partnerships intentionally move beyond coordination toward deeper integration, often redefining roles, decision-making processes, and programmatic boundaries.

Consider the difference: Two food banks may coordinate distribution schedules to avoid overlapping in service areas. That's coordination. But if they co-design a regional hunger strategy, apply for joint grants, and share impact data while centering community voice, they've entered the realm of strategic partnership.

Several motivating factors drive nonprofits to pursue strategic partnerships:

1. **Complexity of the problem:** Social issues such as homelessness or early childhood education are multifaceted and cannot be solved by a single entity. Collaboration becomes a necessity.

2. **Resource constraints:** Pooling administrative functions, co-locating services, or jointly procuring technology platforms can increase efficiency and reduce duplication.

3. **Funders' expectations:** Increasingly, funders reward collaboration over siloed efforts, valuing comprehensive solutions that reflect system-level thinking.

4. **Community voice and equity:** Deep partnerships offer opportunities to include historically marginalized stakeholders in decision-making and leadership roles.

Still, strategic partnerships are not without risk. Poorly structured collaborations can drain time, generate conflict, or blur accountability. Leaders must ensure that partnerships align with mission, values, and organizational capacity. A nonprofit that joins a coalition merely to access new funding without assessing fit or strategic value risks mission drift (Nonprofit Quarterly, 2020).

Successful partnerships begin with clarity: What are we trying to achieve together that we cannot accomplish alone? Who needs to be at the table? How will decisions be made, and how will success be defined and measured?

As we move into Section 8.2, we will explore formal models of partnership that provide structure for answering these questions. Before building a collaboration, leaders must first understand the range of available forms and how each aligns with their strategic goals.

Models of Collaborative Engagement

Not all partnerships are created equal. Some are short-term efforts to co-host an event or share a grant. Others evolve into long-term alliances that reshape entire systems. For nonprofit leaders, understanding the different models of collaboration isn't just an academic exercise; it's essential for choosing the right structure to match your goals, resources, and partners.

Let's start with one of the most structured and ambitious models: collective impact. You may have heard the term; it's gained traction in recent years, especially among funders and policy circles. At its core, collective impact is about multiple organizations coming together to solve complex problems, like early childhood literacy or youth homelessness. What makes it distinct is that it's not just about working in the same space; it's about aligning around a shared agenda, measuring progress with common indicators, and coordinating efforts through a central backbone organization (Kania & Kramer, 2011).

Take the Strive Partnership in Cincinnati. Instead of each school and nonprofit tackling education in isolation, they coordinated cradle-to-career strategies, from early learning to post-secondary success. The result wasn't just better outcomes; it was a restructured system that responded more effectively to the needs of children and families (FSG, 2014).

Of course, collective impact isn't the only game in town. Some collaborations focus less on systemic transformation and more on enabling day-to-day cooperation. This is where backbone organizations come in. These entities, often nonprofits themselves, don't provide direct services. Instead, they support partners by managing logistics, hosting meetings, collecting shared data, and keeping the collaboration on track.

If you've ever worked in a coalition and thought, "We need someone just to keep us organized," that's the role of the backbone. But beware, it takes skill and diplomacy. The backbone must be seen as neutral, trustworthy, and capable of elevating everyone's work without dominating the conversation.

Another increasingly common structure is the public-private partnership, or PPP. These collaborations bring together nonprofits with government agencies or corporate partners to address shared goals (Bryson et al., 2015). You might see this in housing, workforce development, or disaster relief. During the COVID-19 pandemic, for example, cities partnered with nonprofits to distribute meals, provide shelter, or expand testing. In Seattle, the city's Navigation Team worked closely with outreach nonprofits and health agencies to serve people experiencing homelessness in real time.

These partnerships can be powerful, but they can also be fraught. Government timelines don't always match nonprofit realities. Corporations may bring resources, but they also bring different values. Leaders must negotiate terms carefully and stay grounded in their mission, especially when navigating power imbalances or funding dependencies.

Not all partnerships need to be formalized at that level. Some are more fluid - coalitions, federations, and networks often form around advocacy goals, regional identities, or service coordination. For instance, Feeding America operates as a national federation of food banks, offering shared branding and logistical support while allowing local affiliates to retain autonomy. Meanwhile, housing advocates might join a looser statewide coalition to push for rent control or zoning reform, working together when needed but retaining their own identities and strategies.

Finally, some partnerships are built around shared infrastructure. Joint ventures and shared service arrangements allow nonprofits to pool resources, whether it's a shared office, accounting team, or technology platform. This can be especially helpful for small organizations that want to stay lean but also benefit from professionalized systems (Tamarack Institute, 2022).

A youth arts collective in the Midwest offers a compelling example: several small nonprofits co-located in a renovated warehouse, creating a shared public gallery and back-office hub. By doing so, they saved on overhead and created new visibility for their work, something none could have done alone.

Across all these models, one question should guide your decision-making: What are we trying to accomplish together that we cannot do alone? The answer will help you choose the structure, level of formality, and degree of integration that fits your context.

In the next section, we'll dive deeper into what makes these partnerships work, not just on paper, but in practice. Because no matter how well-designed the model, collaboration rises or falls on a single foundation: trust.

Sidebar: Comparing Models of Strategic Collaboration

Model	Purpose & Use Case	Key Characteristics	Risks & Considerations
Collective Impact	Solve complex, systemic problems (e.g., early childhood education, homelessness)	• Shared agenda • Common measurement • Backbone support • Mutually reinforcing activities • Continuous communication	• Requires significant time and trust • Risk of "top-down" leadership if not community-driven
Backbone Organiza-tion	Coordinate and support multiple partners in a shared initiative	• Neutral facilitator • Manages data, meetings, and communication • Supports accountability without delivering services	• Needs clear role boundaries • Risk of perceived power imbalance
Public -Private Partner-ship (PPP)	Leverage cross-sector strengths for service delivery or policy solutions	• Formal agreements • Resource sharing • Joint service design or implementation	• Conflicting values or timelines • Risk of mission drift or dependency

Model	Purpose & Use Case	Key Characteristics	Risks & Considerations
Federation / Coalition	Coordinate advocacy, branding, or service strategies across multiple entities	• Shared identity or policy agenda • Flexible structure (coalitions); more formal compliance (federations)	• Governance complexity • Risk of fragmentation or diluted impact
Joint Venture / Shared Services	Reduce costs or increase capacity by pooling resources	• Shared infrastructure • Joint staffing or admin functions • Often locally focused	• Requires strong agreements • Can blur lines of accountability

Building and Sustaining Trust-Based Partnerships

If structure is the skeleton of collaboration, then trust is the lifeblood. Without it, even the most carefully designed partnership models collapse under the weight of miscommunication, turf battles, or unmet expectations. Trust-based partnerships are not just about being polite or friendly; they are built on mutual accountability, cultural fluency, and a shared commitment to equitable outcomes (Cabaj & Weaver, 2016).

Trust Is Earned, Not Assumed

It's tempting to think that shared mission alone is enough to sustain a partnership. In reality, shared goals often mask deeply different values, operating cultures, and power positions. A large, well-resourced nonprofit might view efficiency as its north star, while a grassroots organization prioritizes community process and voice. Unless these assumptions are named and navigated, they can quietly erode the relationship.

Building trust starts with showing up consistently, transparently, and with humility. That means attending planning meetings even when decisions don't immediately affect your organization. It means sharing data and credit. It also means being willing to acknowledge mistakes and adjust course when something isn't working.

Trust-Building Strategies in Action

Effective trust-building is not accidental; it's the result of deliberate leadership choices. Consider the following real-world examples:

Start with small wins: When a regional health equity coalition in Oregon brought together hospitals, community clinics, and tribal organizations, they began by collaborating on a joint flu shot campaign. It wasn't transformative, but it allowed partners to test the waters, learn each other's communication styles, and build confidence in shared logistics before tackling more sensitive issues like resource allocation or racial disparities in outcomes (Nonprofit Quarterly, 2020).

Make power visible and shared: In one East Coast city, a youth development initiative invited community youth to co-chair advisory committees alongside executive directors. By explicitly sharing decision-making roles, they signaled that lived experience was as valued as institutional credentials. Over time, this fostered deeper trust across generational and racial divides.

Name tensions, then stay at the table: In a housing justice partnership, conflict emerged between organizers focused on direct action and service providers reliant on government contracts. Instead of ignoring the tension, leaders created structured dialogue sessions to surface values, clarify boundaries, and co-design advocacy strategies that respected each party's constraints. Conflict didn't disappear, but trust grew through the shared effort to address it openly.

Cultural Fluency as a Trust Multiplier

Cultural competence, explored in Chapter 1, is not an optional bonus in trust-based partnerships; it is foundational. Language access, recognition of historical trauma, and an awareness of how race, class, or geography shape power in collaboration are all part of this equation (Tamarack Institute, 2022).

When a national education nonprofit launched a partnership with rural school districts in Appalachia, they initially encountered resistance. Locals saw the outsiders as well-meaning but out of touch. It wasn't until the nonprofit hired a regional coordinator from within the community that restructured its planning sessions to reflect local rhythms, and adjusted language to reflect regional idioms that the partnership began to flourish.

Leaders who bring cultural humility and curiosity into cross-sector work help lower defensiveness and increase engagement. As one coalition leader noted, "People don't need you to be perfect. They need to know you're listening and that you're in it for the long haul."

Sustaining Trust Over Time

Trust isn't a one-time achievement; it must be maintained. Leadership transitions, funding changes, or public controversy can all put pressure on even the strongest partnerships. That's why it's essential to build institutional trust, not just interpersonal rapport.

Some proven strategies include:

1. Formalizing shared norms in MOUs or charters, not just tasks and deliverables, but how decisions will be made, who speaks for the group, and how conflicts will be addressed.

2. Building redundancy into relationships so that trust doesn't depend on a single champion. Crosstrain staff, rotate meeting facilitators, and ensure multiple connections across organizations.

3. Regularly evaluating the health of the partnership using structured feedback loops, reflection retreats, or even third-party assessments.

As partnerships mature, governance structures become more important. Who makes decisions? How is authority distributed? What happens when power is unevenly held? In the next section, we'll explore the mechanics of governance, power, and shared decision-making and how to navigate them without compromising equity or impact.

Case Study: From Skepticism to Shared Vision - The "River North Collaborative"

In 2021, five nonprofit organizations serving immigrants and refugees in a mid-sized Midwestern city formed the River North Collaborative. On paper, their missions aligned: housing, legal aid, workforce development, language access, and trauma recovery. But early meetings were tense. Turf concerns surfaced immediately - who would get credit? Would one agency dominate? Was this just another funder-driven hoop?

The turning point came when the group paused operational planning and invested in relationship-building. They held a two-day retreat facilitated by a bilingual mediator, where leaders shared personal stories about why they entered this work. They acknowledged tensions; one director admitted fearing her organization would be "swallowed" by a larger partner. Another shared frustration about always being the "translator" for funders.

From that space of honesty, they co-created a charter that prioritized equity, recognized labor imbalances (like interpretation work), and outlined how community members would co-lead program design. They began rotating meeting facilitators and adopted a "no decisions made without all voices present" rule.

Eighteen months later, River North launched a joint housing stabilization program that leveraged each agency's strengths. More importantly, they built a container of trust sturdy enough to carry them through inevitable disagreements. As one partner said, "We stopped competing for scraps and started building the table together."

Sidebar: Trust-Building Checklist for Nonprofit Leaders

Use this checklist to assess and strengthen trust within new or existing partnerships. Consider revisiting it periodically as relationships evolve.

Practice	Yes	Needs Work
We have established shared goals that are clearly documented and understood by all partners.	☐	☐
All partners have contributed to the design of the collaboration, not just implementation.	☐	☐
We acknowledge and discuss power dynamics openly (e.g., size, funding, history).	☐	☐

Practice	Yes	Needs Work
Our meetings and communications are transparent, inclusive, and frequent.	☐	☐
Cultural differences (language, norms, community values) are respected and integrated into how we work.	☐	☐
We have formal agreements (e.g., MOU) that define roles, responsibilities, and decision-making processes.	☐	☐
There is more than one point of contact between organizations to prevent over-reliance on individuals.	☐	☐
We create space to reflect on what's working and what isn't without fear of retribution.	☐	☐
Community stakeholders, especially those most affected, are involved in shaping the work.	☐	☐
We have a plan to revisit and adjust the partnership as conditions change.	☐	☐

Governance, Power, and Shared Decision-Making

As partnerships mature, they face a pivotal challenge: how to make decisions together in ways that are fair, functional, and aligned with shared values. Governance in collaborative settings is rarely simple. Unlike a traditional nonprofit board or single-agency hierarchy, cross-sector collaborations often involve multiple organizations with different cultures, stakeholders, and accountability structures. Add in differing levels of power - financial, political, cultural - and the risk of imbalance becomes real (Emerson et al., 2012).

What Makes Collaborative Governance Different

Collaborative governance isn't just about who sits at the table; rather, it is about how the table is built, who gets to speak, and what happens when voices disagree. In traditional structures, decision-making flows vertically. In partnerships, however, authority must be shared horizontally, which can feel ambiguous or even risky, especially for organizations used to operating independently.

Consider a citywide youth violence prevention coalition involving public health officials, community organizers, educators, and police. Each partner brings critical expertise but also different sources of power. Without clear structures, meetings can devolve into competing agendas or token consultation.

To avoid this, effective partnerships invest in intentional governance design. That means co-creating decision-making protocols, clarifying roles and responsibilities, and agreeing on how conflict will be addressed. Some groups use consensus-based models; others opt for majority vote or tiered decision rights (e.g., some issues require full agreement, others can be delegated to a subcommittee). There is no universal formula, but the process of co-designing the governance itself builds trust and commitment.

Surfacing and Managing Power Dynamics

Power exists in every partnership, whether acknowledged or not. It shows up in who controls resources, whose data is used, who sets meeting agendas, and whose voices are amplified. Ignoring power dynamics doesn't make them go away; it often reinforces them (Stanford Social Innovation Review, 2021).

Successful collaborations name power explicitly. They ask:

1. Who benefits from this partnership?

2. Who holds decision-making authority and why?

3. Are smaller or grassroots partners fully included in strategic discussions, or just implementation?

4. Are community members treated as stakeholders or co-creators?

A national foundation supporting a food justice network learned this lesson when smaller, BIPOC-led organizations began exiting the partnership. Their feedback revealed that while their labor was used (e.g., community outreach), they had no say in funding decisions. In response, the network paused all new funding disbursements and restructured its governance model to include a participatory budgeting process, giving each partner, regardless of size, a vote in how pooled funds were allocated.

This isn't just about fairness; it's about effectiveness. Partnerships that center equity in governance are more likely to produce lasting, community-rooted solutions.

Tools for Equitable Shared Decision-Making

To support shared governance, nonprofit leaders can implement tools such as:

1. Decision matrices that clarify which types of decisions require full group input versus delegated authority.

2. Facilitated consensus models, like Fist-to-Five voting, to gauge support without silencing dissent.

3. Rotating facilitation to prevent any one organization from setting the tone or pace.

Community advisory councils with real influence, not symbolic roles, especially when the partnership serves historically marginalized groups.

Leaders should also conduct governance audits every 6–12 months to ask: Are we still sharing power as we intended? Who's been added or excluded since we began?

Once governance systems are in place, how do we know whether the partnership is working? Not just at the program level, but in terms of trust, equity, and shared outcomes (Bryson et al., 2015)? In the final section, we'll explore how to evaluate the effectiveness of collaborative efforts and ensure that partnerships remain dynamic, inclusive, and mission-aligned over time.

Sample Governance Structures for Collaborative Partnerships

These simplified models illustrate how different partnerships structure governance. Each approach has trade-offs depending on scale, trust level, and purpose.

Structure	Description	Best For	Risks
Lead Organization Model	One organization serves as the fiscal agent and primary decision-makers; others act as advisors or implementers.	Short-term projects, grant-funded collaboratives, or emergency coalitions.	Can reinforce power imbalances; limits shared ownership.
Steering Committee Model	A representative group with defined seats makes key decisions. Roles and voting processes formalized.	Mid- to large-scale initiatives seeking democratic input with structure.	Risk of tokenism if not all members have real influence.
Consensus Coalition Model	All partners participate in decision-making; consensus is required for major actions.	Values-based collaboratives with high trust and shared mission.	Time-intensive; may stall when disagreements arise.

Structure	Description	Best For	Risks
Community-Governed Model	A council of residents or service users holds governing authority, with organizations acting in support roles.	Place-based partnerships, racial justice work, or community wealth-building models.	Requires deep power-sharing and capacity-building for governance participants.

Worksheet: Collaborative Governance Planning Guide

Use this worksheet to design or refine your partnership's governance structure. These prompts can support initial convenings or mid-course corrections.

Step 1: Clarify Roles

1. Who is leading the coordination?

2. Who controls funding?

3. Who facilitates meetings and sets agendas?

4. Who speaks for the partnership publicly?

Step 2: Define Decision-Making

1. What types of decisions will be made jointly (e.g., budget, strategy, hiring)?

2. What decision-making method will we use? (e.g., majority vote, consensus, rotating vote)

3. How will we document and communicate decisions?

Step 3: Address Power and Equity

1. Are all partners equally resourced to participate (e.g., com-

pensated for time, access to technology)?

2. Are grassroots or frontline partners meaningfully involved in decisions, not just service delivery?

3. How are community voices integrated into governance?

Step 4: Design Accountability Mechanisms

1. Will we develop an MOU or charter to document roles and expectations?

2. How often will we revisit governance to ensure it's still working?

3. What will we do if conflict arises or trust erodes?

Step 5: Build Institutional Redundancy

1. Are leadership roles (e.g., chair, facilitator) shared or rotating?

2. Are there at least two people per organization engaged, in case of turnover?

3. Do we have shared access to critical documents, data, and systems?

Evaluating Collaborative Success

Strategic partnerships are often launched with high hopes and shared intentions, but how do we know if they're working? Unlike individual program evaluations, collaborative success must be assessed on multiple levels: outcomes, equity, trust, governance, and sustainability. Without intentional evaluation, partnerships risk stagnation, mission drift, or erosion of stakeholder confidence (Center for Evaluation Innovation, 2020).

Rethinking What "Success" Means in Collaboration

In collaborative settings, traditional metrics like "number of people served" or "dollars raised" are only part of the story. Equally important are the less visible elements, like how power is distributed, whether trust has deepened, and if the community sees value in the partnership.

Successful partnerships ask hard questions early and often:

1. Are we achieving more together than we could have alone?

2. Are our partners and stakeholders equitably benefiting from the collaboration?

3. Are we holding ourselves accountable to the values we set at the start?

These questions don't lend themselves to simple dashboards, but they can and should be measured.

Case Example 1: Data Sharing as a Measure of Trust

A multi-agency mental health initiative in the Pacific Northwest set out to improve crisis response for unhoused individuals. Initially, each organization tracked client data independently. After months of building rapport and negotiating confidentiality protocols, the group implemented a shared case management platform. While client outcomes were critical, the partnership viewed the ability to co-manage data as its first true indicator of success. Trust had matured to the point where shared accountability was possible.

Case Example 2: Community Ownership as Impact

In a southern U.S. city, a food security partnership between nonprofits, churches, and schools began by distributing boxed meals during the pandemic. Over time, the partnership shifted from "delivering to" the community to "building with" the community. Residents now co-lead planning sessions, and a community advisory board holds veto power over key decisions. While distribution numbers remained flat, donor support doubled and client satisfaction jumped, showing that meaningful engagement, not scale alone, was driving impact.

Key Dimensions of Collaborative Success

The table below outlines multiple dimensions of success, including traditional and equity-centered indicators.

Dimension	Indicators of Success	Sample Questions
Shared Outcomes	Goals are met or exceeded; partners align on success metrics	Are we collectively moving the needle on the problem we set out to solve?
Governance & Decision-Making	Roles are clear; conflict is managed constructively; decisions are timely and inclusive	Do all partners feel they have influence? Are decisions made transparently?
Trust & Relationships	High engagement; low attrition; openness to feedback and adaptation	Are partners engaged? Are difficult issues addressed or avoided?
Equity & Inclusion	Historically excluded groups shape decisions and benefit from outcomes	Who is at the table and who isn't? Are resources equitably distributed?

Dimension	Indicators of Success	Sample Questions
Sustainability	The partnership adapts over time, secures long-term support, and develops leadership depth	Do we have a succession plan? Is this work embedded or personality-driven?

Tools and Methods for Assessment

Evaluating collaborative success doesn't require complex tools, but it does require intention. Common methods include:

1. Partner satisfaction surveys with open-ended questions about voice, equity, and engagement.

2. 360-degree reflection tools that allow each member to evaluate the partnership, not just the outcomes.

3. Community listening sessions to validate whether residents experience positive change.

Scorecards or rubrics to assess governance health, shared leadership, and communication.

Some collaboratives develop a "Partnership Health Index", revisited quarterly or biannually, to flag breakdowns early and keep the work aligned with its core values.

Sustainable partnerships are not self-perpetuating. They require ongoing attention, course correction, and recommitment. Evaluation isn't just a way to report progress; it's how collaborations stay honest, equitable, and mission-aligned over time.

As you apply these tools in your own practice, remember that collaboration is not an event. It's a discipline. And like all disciplines, it gets stronger with regular feedback, transparency, and care.

Toolkit: Evaluating Your Strategic Partnership

Step 1: Conduct a Partnership Reflection Session

Purpose: Create space for honest dialogue about what's working, what's not, and how the partnership can improve.

Facilitation Tips:

1. Include representatives from all partner organizations, not just leadership.

2. Use a neutral facilitator if power dynamics may inhibit candor.

3. Share this toolkit in advance to set expectations.

Step 2: Partnership Self-Assessment Template

Ask each partner organization to complete this template individually before your group session. Responses can be shared anonymously or used as a springboard for discussion.

Prompt

1. What do you believe are this partnership's biggest achievements?

2. Where has the partnership fallen short or encountered challenges?

3. How well do you understand your organization's role and responsibilities in the partnership?

4. To what extent do you feel your organization's voice is heard and valued in decision-making?

5.   Do you trust other members of the partnership to follow through on commitments? Why or why not?

6.   Are the benefits of participating in this partnership worth the time and resources invested?

7.   What's one change that would strengthen this partnership moving forward?

Step 3: Partnership Health Rubric

Rate your partnership across five key dimensions using a 1–5 scale, where 1 = Needs Significant Improvement and 5 = Strong/Consistently Evident.

Dimension

1.   **Shared Goals:** Partners are aligned on mission, objectives, and intended outcomes.

2.   **Inclusive Governance:** Roles, responsibilities, and decision-making structures are clear and equitable.

3.   **Trust & Communication:** Information flows freely; partners are open and honest.

4.   **Equity & Representation:** Community voices and under-represented groups have meaningful influence.

5.   **Sustainability & Adaptability:** The collaboration is resilient, with long-term potential beyond current funding.

Optional Scoring Guide:

1.   **21–25** = High-functioning, sustainable partnership

2.   **16–20** = Generally strong, with areas for growth

3.   **11–15** = Mixed performance; requires focused attention

4.   **<10** = At risk; consider redesign or re-commitment

Step 4: Action Planning

Use insights from your assessments to generate next steps:

1. What Needs Strengthening?

2. Proposed Action Who's Responsible?

3. By When?

Optional Add-Ons

1. **Partner Exit Survey:** For departing members to offer feedback and closure

2. **Quarterly Check-In Form:** Short-form version for frequent health monitoring

3. **Partnership Charter Template:** Use when forming new collaboratives or re-launching efforts

In a world of intersecting challenges - homelessness, systemic racism, climate instability, public health disparities - no single organization can create lasting change in isolation. Strategic partnerships have emerged not as a luxury, but as a necessity for mission-driven impact.

Throughout this chapter, we examined the nature and purpose of collaboration in the nonprofit sector. We began by defining what strategic partnerships are, and what they are not, distinguishing them from informal coordination or competitive coexistence. We explored various models of collaborative engagement, from backbone-supported collective impact frameworks to public-private partnerships and shared service ventures. Real-world case examples illustrate how structure must be paired with intention.

As partnerships deepen, trust becomes the glue that binds diverse stakeholders. We emphasized that trust is built not through statements of shared vision alone, but through consistent behavior: transparency, accountability, cultural fluency, and inclusive governance. These dynamics are especially critical in multistakeholder work, where power imbalances, differing worldviews, and resource disparities often complicate collaboration.

We also examined governance structures and shared decision-making models, recognizing that effective partnerships require more than goodwill; they need clarity, processes, and a deep commitment to equity. Finally, we outlined tools and frameworks for evaluating collaborative health and impact, underscoring that sustainable partnerships must be assessed not only on outputs, but also on how well they honor trust, distribute power, and center the voices of those most affected.

As you reflect on this chapter, consider the partnerships your organization is part of or hopes to build. Are they transactional or transformational? Do they reflect your mission and values? Are they helping you do more, or simply doing more of the same?

Strategic collaboration is not a shortcut to impact. It is a discipline that demands care, courage, and ongoing recalibration. But when done well, it can amplify voice, mobilize resources, and shift entire systems toward justice and lasting change.

Discussion Questions

1. Think of a partnership your organization is currently part of or has considered. How would you evaluate whether it is strategic, collaborative, or simply coordinated?

2. What factors should nonprofit leaders weigh before entering

a formal partnership or joint initiative?

3. In your organization, what practices help build or erode trust among external partners?

4. How are decisions currently made in your collaborative efforts? What could be done to make that process more equitable or transparent?

5. Of the collaboration models discussed in this chapter, which one seems most applicable to your organization's goals? Why?

6. What indicators would you use to assess whether a partnership is achieving both impact and equity?

Field Markers

1. **Backbone Organization:** A dedicated entity that provides coordination, data management, and facilitation support for a collective initiative without directly delivering services.

2. **Coalition:** A group of organizations or individuals that voluntarily come together to pursue a shared advocacy or programmatic goal, typically with flexible or informal governance.

3. **Collective Impact:** A structured approach to cross-sector collaboration in which organizations commit to a common agenda, shared measurement, and coordinated actions to address a complex social issue.

4. **Collaborative Governance:** A model of decision-making in which multiple organizations or stakeholders share authority and responsibility for guiding a partnership or initiative.

5. **Consensus Decision-Making:** A process in which all

participants work toward general agreement, often requiring deliberation and compromise to achieve shared outcomes.

6. **Cross-Sector Collaboration:** Partnerships involving entities from different sectors, nonprofit, government, private, and community, to address systemic challenges through shared strategies and pooled resources.

7. **Equity-Centered Evaluation:** An assessment approach that emphasizes power-sharing, community voice, and justice in determining whether partnerships are effective and inclusive.

8. **Federation:** A network of semi-autonomous organizations operating under a shared brand or mission with coordinated standards, services, or advocacy efforts.

9. **Governance Structure:** The formal or informal system through which roles, responsibilities, and decision-making processes are defined and managed in a partnership.

10. **Memorandum of Understanding (MOU):** A written agreement outlining the roles, expectations, and commitments of each party in a collaborative effort, typically used in lieu of legal contracts.

11. **Participatory Decision-Making:** An approach that ensures affected stakeholders, particularly those with lived experience, have meaningful influence in shaping policies, programs, or strategies.

12. **Public-Private Partnership (PPP):** A formalized collaboration between nonprofit organizations and government or corporate entities designed to deliver services or address policy goals.

13. **Shared Measurement System:** A set of agreed-upon indicators and data practices that partners use collectively to track progress and evaluate impact across organizations.

14. **Strategic Partnership:** A formal or semi-formal alliance between organizations designed to advance mutual goals through shared resources, responsibilities, and decision-making authority.

15. **Trust-Based Partnership:** A relationship among collaborators grounded in transparency, mutual respect, open communication, and shared commitment to equitable outcomes.

Epilogue: Leading Forward

Nonprofit leadership is not a fixed destination. It is a continuous process of learning, adaptation, and commitment to mission, to community, and equity. By now, you've engaged with the foundational skills and strategic frameworks that define effective nonprofit leadership. You've examined what it means to lead ethically, collaborate across boundaries, measure what matters, and plan for change in a world that doesn't stand still.

This book began by grounding you in the purpose and complexity of the nonprofit sector. From there, we explored the building blocks of strong leadership: vision, integrity, cultural competence, financial stewardship, program design, evaluation, and strategic collaboration. Along the way, you've encountered case examples, critical tools, and real-world scenarios intended not just to inform but to challenge and equip you for real-world effectiveness.

But no framework, model, or checklist can substitute for the deep work of reflection. Leadership is as much about self-awareness as it is about systems. As you look ahead, consider:

1. What do you want your leadership legacy to be?

2. How will you cultivate your individual sustainability, not just your organization's?

3. What risks are you willing to take to advance justice, inclusion, and innovation in your field?

This work can be lonely. It can also be deeply rewarding. Building a personal leadership brand, one rooted in transparency, humility, and action, takes time. It brings clarity of purpose. And it takes community. Surround yourself with trusted peers, mentors, and emerging leaders.

Share what you learn. Invite feedback. Stay curious.

Whether you're stepping into your first leadership role, deepening your practice, or mentoring the next generation, remember: you don't lead alone. You lead with and through others. And when that leadership is grounded in values, strategy, and reflection, it becomes a force for real and lasting change.

So, take what you've learned here, and lead forward with purpose, with courage, and with care.

References

Anderson, A. A. (2005). The community builder's approach to theory of change: A practical guide to theory development. Aspen Institute.

Anderson, A. A. (2005). The community builder's approach to theory of change: A practical guide to theory development. Aspen Institute. https://www.theoryofchange.org/pdf/TOC_fac_guide.pdf

Anheier, H. K. (2014). Nonprofit organizations: Theory, management, policy (2nd ed.). Routledge.

Association of Fundraising Professionals. (2023). Donor stewardship strategies: Building lasting relationships.

Bamberger, M., Rugh, J., & Mabry, L. (2019). RealWorld evaluation: Working under budget, time, data, and political constraints (3rd ed.). SAGE Publications.

Bass, B. M., & Avolio, B. J. (1994). Improving organizational effectiveness through transformational leadership. SAGE Publications.

Bebbington, A., & Thiele, G. (1993). Non-governmental organizations and the state in Latin America: Rethinking roles in sustainable agricultural development. Routledge.

Blackbaud Institute. (2022). The donor retention playbook: Metrics and methods for long-term success. https://institute.blackbaud.com

BoardSource. (2021). Leading with intent: BoardSource index of nonprofit board practices.

BoardSource. (2022). Leading with intent: Ethics in nonprofit governance.

BoardSource. (2023). Race to lead: Revisited.

Bradshaw, J. (1972). A taxonomy of social need. New Society, 30(3), 640–643.

Bremner, R. H. (1988). American philanthropy. University of Chicago Press.

Bridges, W. (2009). Managing transitions: Making the most of change (3rd ed.). Da Capo Press.

Bridgespan Group. (2021). Tools for assessing and mitigating nonprofit risk.

Bridgespan Group. (2022). Adaptive leadership in uncertainty.

Bryson, J. M. (2018). Strategic planning for public and nonprofit organizations (5th ed.). Jossey-Bass.

Bryson, J. M. (2021). Strategic planning for public and nonprofit organizations (6th ed.). Wiley.

Bryson, J. M., Crosby, B. C., & Bloomberg, L. (2014). Public value governance: Moving beyond traditional public administration and the new public management. Public Administration Review, 74(4), 445–456. https://doi.org/10.1111/puar.12238

Bryson, J. M., Crosby, B. C., & Stone, M. M. (2015). Designing and implementing cross-sector collaborations: Needed and challenging. Public Administration Review, 75(5), 647–663. https://doi.org/10.1111/puar.12432

Burnes, B. (2004). Kurt Lewin and the planned approach to change: A re-appraisal. Journal of Management Studies, 41(6), 977–1002. https://doi.org/10.1111/j.1467-6486.2004.00463.x

Burnett, K. (2021). Relationship fundraising: A donor-based approach to the business of raising money (3rd ed.). Wiley.

Burns, J. M. (1978). Leadership. Harper & Row.

Cabaj, M., & Weaver, L. (2016). Collective impact 3.0: An evolving framework for community change. Tamarack Institute. https://www.tamarackcommunity.ca/library/collective-impact-3.0

Cargo, M., & Mercer, S. L. (2008). The value and challenges of participatory research: Strengthening its practice. Annual Review of Public Health, 29(1), 325–350.

Center for Community Health and Development. (2023). Community

Tool Box. University of Kansas.

Center for Effective Philanthropy. (2022). Making evaluation meaningful.

Center for Evaluation Innovation. (2020). Equitable evaluation framework™. https://www.equitableeval.org

Charitable Giving Research Center. (2022). Effective practices in nonprofit crowdfunding.

Charity Navigator. (2023). DEI metrics for nonprofits.

Child Trends. (2024). Open data portals and donor engagement: An internal evaluation report.

Chilisa, B. (2012). Indigenous research methodologies. SAGE Publications.

Climate Impact Lab. (2022). Extreme heat and urban vulnerability: A case study of the 2021 Pacific Northwest heat wave.

Community-Centric Fundraising. (2023). The principles of community-centric fundraising.

Connell, J. P., & Kubisch, A. C. (1998). Applying a theory of change approach to the evaluation of comprehensive community initiatives: Progress, prospects, and problems. The Aspen Institute.

Cooperrider, D. L., & Whitney, D. (2005). Appreciative inquiry: A positive revolution in change. Berrett-Koehler.

Coulton, C. J., Chan, T., & Mikelbank, K. (2011). Finding place in community change initiatives: Using GIS to uncover resident perceptions of their neighborhoods. Journal of Community Practice, 19(1), 10–28.

Council on Foundations. (2023). Next generation philanthropy: Trends and tools for CSR engagement.

Council on Foundations. (2023). Next generation philanthropy: Trends and tools for Gen Z donors.

Creswell, J. W., & Plano Clark, V. L. (2017). Designing and conducting mixed methods research (3rd ed.). SAGE Publications.

Crutchfield, L., & Grant, H. (2012). Forces for good: The six practices of high-impact nonprofits (Rev. ed.). Jossey-Bass.

Dean-Coffey, D. (2018). What's race got to do with it? Equity and philanthropic evaluation practice. American Journal of Evaluation, 39(4), 527–542.

Deloitte. (2022). Nonprofit technology trends: Adapting to crisis-driven change.

Deloitte. (2022). Purpose-driven businesses and the rise of stakeholder capitalism.

Dillman, D. A., Smyth, J. D., & Christian, L. M. (2014). Internet, phone, mail, and mixed-mode surveys: The tailored design method (4th ed.). Wiley.

Doran, G. T. (1981). There's a S.M.A.R.T. way to write management's goals and objectives. Management Review, 70(11), 35–36.

Ebrahim, A. (2019). Measuring social change: Performance and accountability in a complex world. Stanford University Press.

Ebrahim, A., & Rangan, V. K. (2014). What impact? A framework for measuring the scale and scope of social performance. California Management Review, 56(3), 118–141.

Edelman. (2023). Edelman trust barometer 2023.

Edelman. (2023). Trust barometer special report: Business and society.

Edelman. (2023). Trust barometer special report: Nonprofits.

Edmondson, A. (1999). Psychological safety and learning behavior in work teams. Administrative Science Quarterly, 44(2), 350–383. https://doi.org/10.2307/2666999

Edmondson, A. (2019). The fearless organization: Creating psychological safety in the workplace for learning, innovation, and growth. Wiley.

Emerson, J., & Twersky, F. (2018). The nonprofit lifecycle: Stage-based wisdom for nonprofit capacity. Roberts Foundation.

Emerson, K., Nabatchi, T., & Balogh, S. (2012). An integrative framework for collaborative governance. Journal of Public Administration Research and Theory, 22(1), 1–29. https://doi.org/10.1093/jopart/mur011

Feeding America. (2021). Annual report 2021.

Feeding America. (2021). Responding to a crisis: COVID-19 report on food bank adaptations.

FEMA. (2023). Hurricane Ian response report.

Fitzpatrick, J. L., Sanders, J. R., & Worthen, B. R. (2011). Program evaluation: Alternative approaches and practical guidelines (4th ed.). Pearson Education.

Fowler, A. (2000). NGO futures: Beyond aid: NGDO values and the fourth position. Third World Quarterly, 21(4), 589–603.

FSG. (2014). Backbone starter guide: A summary of major resources about the backbone role in collective impact. https://www.fsg.org/resource/backbone-starter-guide/

Fundraising Effectiveness Project. (2023). 2023 annual report on fundraising trends and retention.

Gallup. (2023). State of the nonprofit workplace.

GEO. (2022). Centering impact in donor communications. Grantmakers for Effective Organizations.

Gienapp, A. (2015). Strategic learning in practice: Tools to create the space & structure for learning. Center for Evaluation Innovation.

Global Cyber Alliance. (2023). Cybersecurity in the nonprofit sector: Risks and solutions.

Goodman, J. (2017). Telling your impact story: A guide to strategic communication for nonprofits. The Communications Network.

Grantmakers for Effective Organizations. (2022). Scaling what works: Sustainability planning for grantees.

Green, L. W., & Kreuter, M. W. (2005). Health program planning: An educational and ecological approach (4th ed.). McGraw-Hill.

Guijt, I. (2014). Participatory approaches: Methodological briefs—impact evaluation no. 5. UNICEF Office of Research.

Guo, C., & Saxton, G. D. (2010). Voice-in, voice-out: Constituent participation and nonprofit advocacy. Nonprofit Policy Forum, 1(1), Article 5. https://doi.org/10.2202/2154-3348.1004

Gupta, J., Fawcett, S., & Valdovinos, M. (2022). Participatory evaluation and community voice in needs assessments. Journal of Community Engagement and Scholarship, 15(2), 88–102.

Gupta, J., Hackett, K., & Ekwaru, J. P. (2022). From knowledge to action: Mobilizing data for equity-focused program implementation. Evaluation and Program Planning, 94, 102117.

Hale, J. (2018). Nonprofit performance management: Using data to measure and improve impact. CharityChannel Press.

Hall, P. D. (2006). A historical overview of philanthropy, voluntary associations, and nonprofit organizations in the United States, 1600–2000. In W. W. Powell & R. Steinberg (Eds.), The nonprofit sector: A research handbook (pp. 32–65). Yale University Press.

Harvard Business Review. (2020). The EQ difference in nonprofits.

Harvard Business Review. (2020). The hard side of change management.

Hatry, H. P. (2006). Performance measurement: Getting results (2nd ed.). The Urban Institute Press.

Heifetz, R., Grashow, A., & Linsky, M. (2009). The practice of adaptive leadership: Tools and tactics for changing your organization and the world. Harvard Business Press.

Herman, R. D., & Renz, D. O. (2020). Advancing nonprofit organizational effectiveness research and practice. Nonprofit Management & Leadership, 31(1), 5–26.

Hiatt, J. (2006). ADKAR: A model for change in business, government and our community. Prosci Learning Center Publications.

IDEO.org. (2015). The field guide to human-centered design. https://www.designkit.org/resources/1

Impact Mapper. (2022). Visualizing impact: Tools for nonprofit data communication. https://www.impactmapper.com

Independent Sector. (2021). Health of the U.S. nonprofit sector: Annual review.

Independent Sector. (2023). Nonprofit ethics toolkit.

Independent Sector. (2023). Risk management and legal compliance for nonprofits.

IRS. (2023). Form 990 instructions: Reporting requirements for tax-exempt organizations. https://www.irs.gov

Israel, B. A., Eng, E., Schulz, A. J., & Parker, E. A. (Eds.). (2013). Methods for community-based participatory research for health (2nd ed.). Jossey-Bass.

Johns Hopkins. (2023). Weekly crisis communication and donor retention study.

Kania, J., & Kramer, M. (2011). Collective impact. Stanford Social Innovation Review, 9(1), 36–41.

Kania, J., & Kramer, M. (2011). Collective impact. Stanford Social Innovation Review, 9(1), 36–41. https://ssir.org/articles/entry/collective_impact

Kania, J., Kramer, M., & Senge, P. (2022). The water of systems change. FSG. https://www.fsg.org/resource/water_of_systems_change

Keleher, T. (2020). Equity audits: Tools for examining institutional bias. Race Forward.

Kettner, P. M., Moroney, R. M., & Martin, L. L. (2017). Designing and managing programs: An effectiveness-based approach (5th ed.). SAGE Publications.

Kim, W. C., & Mauborgne, R. (2015). Blue ocean strategy: How to create uncontested market space and make the competition irrelevant (Expanded ed.). Harvard Business Review Press.

Kirkpatrick, D. L., & Kirkpatrick, J. D. (2006). Evaluating training programs: The four levels (3rd ed.). Berrett-Koehler Publishers.

Kirkpatrick, J. D., & Kirkpatrick, W. K. (2016). Four levels of training evaluation. ATD Press.

Knowlton, L. W., & Phillips, C. C. (2012). The logic model guidebook: Better strategies for great results (2nd ed.). SAGE Publications.

Kotter, J. P. (2012). Leading change (Rev. ed.). Harvard Business Review Press.

Kretzmann, J. P., & McKnight, J. L. (1993). Building communities from the inside out: A path toward finding and mobilizing a community's assets. ACTA Publications.

Krueger, R. A., & Casey, M. A. (2015). Focus groups: A practical guide for applied research (5th ed.). SAGE Publications.

LaFrance, J., & Nichols, R. (2010). Reframing evaluation: Defining an Indigenous evaluation framework. Canadian Journal of Program Evaluation, 23(2), 13–31.

Lilly Family School of Philanthropy. (2023). Trends in American giving: Annual report on donor behavior. Indiana University. https://philanthropy.iupui.edu

Lines, R. (2004). Influence of participation in strategic change: Resistance, organizational commitment and change goal achievement. Journal of Change Management, 4(3), 193–215. https://doi.org/10.1080/14 69701042000221695

M+R Benchmarks. (2023). 2023 M+R benchmarks study: Digital trends in nonprofit fundraising and advocacy.

McKinsey & Company. (2021). Nonprofits and the COVID-19 crisis: Lessons in resilience.

McKnight, J., & Kretzmann, J. (1996). Mapping community capacity. The Asset-Based Community Development Institute, Northwestern University.

Millesen, J. L., & Carman, J. G. (2022). Budgeting for nonprofit effectiveness. Journal of Nonprofit Education and Leadership, 12(1), 51–67. https://doi.org/10.18666/JNEL-2022-V12-I1-11180

Millesen, J. L., & Carman, J. G. (2022). Budgeting for nonprofit effectiveness. Journal of Nonprofit Education and Leadership, 12(1).

Minkler, M., & Wallerstein, N. (Eds.). (2008). Community-based participatory research for health: From process to outcomes (2nd ed.). Jossey-Bass.

Morariu, J., Athanasiades, K., & Gardner, K. (2013). State of evaluation 2012: Evaluation practice and capacity in the nonprofit sector. Innovation Network.

National Civic League. (2021). Promising practices in community engagement.

National Committee for Responsive Philanthropy. (2023). Equity in fundraising: Case studies and benchmarks.

National Council of Nonprofits. (2021). Diversity, equity, and inclusion in nonprofit organizations: Survey findings.

National Council of Nonprofits. (2022). Partnering with government: How nonprofits work with government and what needs to change. https://www.councilofnonprofits.org

National Council of Nonprofits. (2023). Diversity in the nonprofit sector.

National Council of Nonprofits. (2023). Mission-driven budgeting: A guide to financial storytelling. https://www.councilofnonprofits.org

National Council of Nonprofits. (2023). Multi-year budgeting: A guide to long-term financial health. https://www.councilofnonprofits.org

National Council of Nonprofits. (2023). Nonprofit budgeting: A practical guide. https://www.councilofnonprofits.org

National Council of Nonprofits. (2023). Scenario planning for nonprofits: A practical guide. https://www.councilofnonprofits.org

National Council of Nonprofits. (2023a). Equity in practice: Nonprofit approaches to needs assessment.

National Council of Nonprofits. (2023b). Managing risk in a changing nonprofit environment.

National Council of Nonprofits. (2023c). Mission-driven budgeting: A guide to financial storytelling.

National Council of Nonprofits. (2023d). Sustaining impact: Financial and strategic planning for nonprofits.

Netting, F. E., O'Connor, M. K., & Fauri, D. P. (2008). Comparative approaches to program planning. Wiley.

Nicholls, J., Lawlor, E., Neitzert, E., & Goodspeed, T. (2012). A guide to social return on investment. The SROI Network.

Nonprofit Finance Fund. (2022). Adapting to uncertainty: Lessons from nonprofit scenario planning. https://nff.org

Nonprofit Finance Fund. (2022). State of the sector: Financial planning in uncertain times.

Nonprofit Finance Fund. (2022). State of the sector: Financial planning in uncertain times. https://nff.org

Nonprofit HR. (2023). Workforce trends report.

Nonprofit Quarterly. (2020). Rethinking nonprofit collaboration: Equity, trust, and power dynamics. https://nonprofitquarterly.org

Nonprofit Quarterly. (2021). Best practices in ethics training.

Nonprofit Quarterly. (2022). Ethical leadership in times of crisis.

Nonprofit Tech for Good. (2022). Global trends in nonprofit communications. https://www.nptechforgood.com

Nonprofit Tech for Good. (2023). Global nonprofit technology report: Mobile giving and donor trends.

Nonprofit Tech for Good. (2023). Nonprofit tech trends 2023.

NTEN. (2023). Nonprofit technology trends report: Bridging the digital divide.

NTEN. (2023). Technology investment and compliance efficiency in nonprofits.

Patton, M. Q. (2011). Developmental evaluation: Applying complexity concepts to enhance innovation and use. Guilford Press.

Patton, M. Q. (2015). Qualitative research & evaluation methods (4th ed.). SAGE Publications.

Preskill, H., & Gopal, S. (2014). Evaluating complexity: Propositions for improving practice. FSG.

Preskill, H., & Torres, R. T. (1999). Evaluative inquiry for learning in organizations. SAGE Publications.

Public Profit. (2015). Youth participatory evaluation: Strategies for engaging young people.

Race to Lead Initiative. (2022). Still leading in the margins: BIPOC nonprofit leaders on funding, trust, and equity. Building Movement Project.

Rainie, S. C., Rodriguez-Lonebear, D., & Martinez, A. (2017). Data sovereignty and Indigenous peoples. In T. Kukutai & J. Taylor (Eds.), Indigenous data sovereignty: Toward an agenda (pp. 293–309). ANU Press.

Ready.gov. (2023). Annual emergency preparedness benchmarking report.

Ross, T. (2020). Seeing the whole student: A guide to equity-centered evaluation in education. National Equity Project.

Salamon, L. M. (2012). America's nonprofit sector: A primer (3rd ed.). Foundation Center.

Salamon, L. M. (2017). The resilient sector revisited. Brookings Institution Press.

Salamon, L. M. (2017). The resilient sector revisited: The new challenge to nonprofit America. Brookings Institution Press.

Salamon, L. M., & Sokolowski, S. W. (2016). Beyond nonprofits: Re-conceptualizing the third sector. Voluntas: International Journal of Voluntary and Nonprofit Organizations, 27(4), 1515–1545.

Saldaña, J. (2021). The coding manual for qualitative researchers (4th ed.). SAGE Publications.

Saldaña, J., Leavy, P., & Beretvas, S. N. (2021). Fundamentals of qualitative research (2nd ed.). Oxford University Press.

Sargeant, A., & Shang, J. (2016). Fundraising principles and practice. Jossey-Bass.

Schwarzer, R., & Jerusalem, M. (1995). Generalized self-efficacy scale. In J. Weinman, S. Wright, & M. Johnston (Eds.), Measures in health psychology: A user's portfolio. NFER-Nelson.

Smartsheet. (2023). Project management for nonprofits: Tools, tips, and templates.

Social Enterprise Alliance. (2022). The state of social enterprise in the U.S.

Sontag-Padilla, L. M., Staplefoote, B. L., & Gonzalez Morgan, C. (2022). Nonprofit leadership in a crisis: Lessons from COVID-19 (Research Report RRA500-1). RAND Corporation.

Stanford Social Innovation Review. (2021). Collaborative crisis response: A new playbook for nonprofits.

Stanford Social Innovation Review. (2021). Power in partnerships: Building equitable collaborations. https://ssir.org/articles/entry/power_in_partnerships

Stanford Social Innovation Review. (2022). Digital advocacy: Strategies for building movements online.

Stanford Social Innovation Review. (2023). The cost of mission drift.

Stanford Social Innovation Review. (2023). The donor shift: Why financial storytelling drives retention. https://ssir.org

Stanford Social Innovation Review. (2024). Authentic voices: Coauthoring impact narratives with beneficiaries. Stanford Social Innovation Review, 22(1), 45–50.

Tamarack Institute. (2022). Measuring collaboration: Equity-centered approaches to evaluation. https://www.tamarackcommunity.ca

Tech Impact. (2023). The nonprofit guide to AI and automation tools.

TechSoup. (2023). Data-driven nonprofits: Case studies in impact measurement.

TechSoup. (2024). AI and automation in the nonprofit sector: Adoption patterns and risks.

Tempel, E. R., Seiler, T. L., & Burlingame, D. F. (2016). Achieving excellence in fundraising (4th ed.). Wiley.

Trello. (2022). Nonprofit collaboration guide.

U.S. Department of Energy. (2023). Inflation Reduction Act: Clean energy funding opportunities for community-based organizations.

U.S. Global Change Research Program. (2023). National climate assessment: Nonprofit infrastructure risk zones.

Urban Institute. (2022). Nonprofit sector's economic impact.

Urban Institute. (2022). Participatory assessment practices in community-based organizations.

Urban Institute. (2022). The nonprofit sector in brief 2022.

Urban Institute. (2024). Human services nonprofits and structural poverty: Organizational adaptations.

Villanueva, E. (2018). Decolonizing wealth: Indigenous wisdom to heal divides and restore balance. Berrett-Koehler.

W.K. Kellogg Foundation. (2017). The step-by-step guide to evaluation: How to become savvy evaluation consumers.

W.K. Kellogg Foundation. (2020). Step-by-step guide to evaluation.

W.K. Kellogg Foundation. (2020a). Evaluation handbook.

W.K. Kellogg Foundation. (2020b). Logic model development guide.

Wang, C. C., & Burris, M. A. (1997). Photovoice: Concept, methodology, and use for participatory needs assessment. Health Education & Behavior, 24(3), 369–387.

Washington State Department of Social and Health Services. (2023). Provider and services contracting. https://www.dshs.wa.gov

World Economic Forum. (2024). Leapfrogging development: Innovation in the Global South.

World Health Organization. (2023). Global health statistics.

World Health Organization. (2023). Nonprofits in global health.

About the Author

Holly Morgan is an accomplished executive leader with over 30 years of experience guiding community-based programs, nonprofit organizations, and human service initiatives. She currently serves as Executive Director at OlyCAP in Port Townsend, WA, where she leads efforts in community empowerment and social service delivery.

www.ingramcontent.com/pod-product-compliance
Lightning Source LLC
Chambersburg PA
CBHW061622250726

48659CB00004B/1044